PRAISE FOR TROY
ETERNAL IMPACT

"Troy has lived a true rags-to-riches story of trial and triumph. Break this book open and break through to your true potential."

—Alan Hobson, two-time cancer survivor, Mt. Everest climber and summiteer, best-selling author of *Cancer Survivorship from the Inside Out* and *Climb Back from Cancer* (www.SurviveCANcer.ca)

———

"Authentic and straight from the heart! Thank you for the masterpiece, Troy. Inspiring and real! Relevant lessons for today's leaders!"

—David Horsager, CEO of Trust Edge Leadership Institute; best-selling author

———

"Eternal Impact is not just another book on how to be a better leader. Troy takes you on a very vulnerable and introspective journey through nine key themes that certainly had this reader pausing to reflect on so many occasions from cover to cover."

—Troy Hazard, serial entrepreneur, speaker, and Amazon best-selling business author

———

"Troy Nix has written a truly inspiring book that will impact your life and touch your heart. Full of real-world anecdotes and delivered with passion, this awe-inspiring piece will get you to rethink your perspective on the things you do every day and will inspire you to build more authentic relationships both in and out of work. I've read dozens of memoirs and leadership books, but this one I'll be sure to buy for others. You should too!"

—Lt. Col. Waldo Waldman, author of the *New York Times* bestseller *Never Fly Solo*

"Having witnessed his enthusiasm, habits, and leadership firsthand, this book is a must-read for those who want to truly grow their level of positive impact on others. The energy and enthusiasm you sense when you read the book reflects the man himself. Compelling, witty, and self-deprecating, Troy Nix's memoir measures up to the lofty standard he sets for himself and that others should live by."

—H. Alan Rothenbuecher, partner at Benesch,
Friedlander, Coplan & Aronoff LLP

———

"Troy takes the reader on a growth journey, guiding us toward transformational leadership and the best version of ourselves. His story is one of overcoming obstacles, starting with his humble beginnings and finding his own transformation into a successful businessman. Through his engaging and genuine style, we learn how to empower and motivate a team to achieve greater goals together, as each member reaches their individual full potential. A wonderful read!"

—Thomas M. Dafnos, managing partner of Crosspoint Wealth Advisors

———

"Troy Nix has written an amazing piece of work on living an impactful life. Since the first day I met Troy, his contagious excitement, his passion for people and life, and my connection to his values as a leader have changed my life. I have learned so much from him, but reading this book puts it all in perspective. We only live one time, and if you want to live a life that makes a difference and influences those around you, then this book is a must-read. You will be captivated from page one all the way to the end. Troy's experiences will make you think and develop the skills to help you make an impact!"

—Laurie Harbour, president and CEO of Harbour Results, Inc.

"*Troy is in the realm beyond vulnerability. That's the price of admission to be a loving human being who is driven to make an impact. He shares his story to draw out timeless principles that must be lived, to be a leader of impact. You read his book, you hear him speak, you experience passion and inspiration firsthand. You now know it's possible. Troy and his book are a calling and a reminder—to make an impact, you must not only be devoted to performance, you must be devoted to human beings. This devotion, I dare say, is wholly absent in many businesses—it's up to you, not him, to bring it back. And you bring it back by the courage to lead human beings. And when you lead human beings, you most certainly will make an impact. Troy, by his example, demonstrates the fruits of this impact—sheer joy, meaning, and purpose. Thank you for writing this book.*"

—Ryan Krupa, cofounder of MOSAIC, author of *The Gospel of Leadership*

———

"*My first meeting with Troy was in my office. He was making a cold call selling me on the idea of putting together a group of businesspeople to share ideas on how to recruit and train employees. Business was strong in those days, but it was difficult to find and keep good employees. Troy was compassionate and convincing, but you could tell he was not in his comfort zone. However, there was something that everyone soon picks up. Troy really believes in what he is doing, and he ignites you with his excitement and enthusiasm. Before long, you can't help yourself. His excitement is contagious, and you are soon on his team and part of his mission. I assure you, as you read this book, you too will feel the excitement. There is no more reward than what comes from helping others. Troy believes in helping others achieve their goals. He wrote this book to extend his reach and share his passion of living a life worth living.*"

—Lindsey Hahn, CEO of Metro Plastics Technologies

"*After reading* Eternal Impact *I'm impressed and thrilled that Troy decided to tell his story and share his life experiences of the concept that it's everyone's social responsibility to do what they can to help their 'fellow man.' Troy, a respected, passionate, and high-energy leader, is uniquely qualified to teach us how to make a positive impact during our lifetime on earth. This book is a must-read that demonstrates what it takes!*"

—Rae S. Gold, industrial engineer, project management professional

ETERNAL
IMPACT

ETERNAL
IMPACT

INSPIRE GREATNESS
IN YOURSELF AND OTHERS

TROY NIX

Advantage®

Advantage Media Group is proud to be a part of the Tree Neutral® program. Tree Neutral offsets the number of trees consumed in the production and printing of this book by taking proactive steps such as planting trees in direct proportion to the number of trees used to print books. To learn more about Tree Neutral, please visit www.treeneutral.com.

Advantage Media Group is a publisher of business, self-improvement, and professional development books and online learning. We help entrepreneurs, business leaders, and professionals share their Stories, Passion, and Knowledge to help others Learn & Grow. Do you have a manuscript or book idea that you would like us to consider for publishing? Please visit **advantagefamily.com** or call **1.866.775.1696**.

*To those who consciously work to positively impact
the lives of others: keep up the good fight because
you are making the world a better place.*

CONTENTS

ACKNOWLEDGMENTS

I would not be where I am today without the help and love of the following close family members and colleagues:

My business mentor and friend, Lindsey Hahn. Thank you for accepting to meet with me in the winter of 1994. Never in my wildest dreams did I envision that meeting turning into a lifelong friendship. I look up to you and respect you!

My mother-in-law, Jane, who is probably reading a book in heaven at this very moment. I just wanted to tell you that I listened to your advice!

Robert Kloepping, the pastor in Fort Wayne, Indiana, who presided over my father-in-law's funeral. I am forever indebted to your sermon; your words significantly altered my life's course and allowed me to understand how common people can uncommonly impact others.

My daughter Laura and son, Daniel. Thank you for your support and for allowing me to use your life's struggles and your accomplishments to inspire others to push the dial forward. I insanely love both of you!

My daughter Maria. Thank you for all of your encouragement and for being my sounding board. Without you, my self-doubt would have gotten the best of me, and you wouldn't be reading this today. I appreciate and love you more than you will ever know.

My wife, Ann. Thank you for wearing that leopard-skin bikini while cleaning the leaves out of your grandmother's gutters when you were fifteen years old; I'm so glad I took the bait! Thank you for always being there for me and for helping me extract the courage to drive forward in this journey. You are the love of my life.

INTRODUCTION
WHO AM I TO WRITE A BOOK?

As is obvious to anyone who reads, the time and effort required to write a book is immense. Although I feel the majority of authors are very confident about sharing their ideas, it took me many years to gain the confidence needed to take this step. The reason I hesitated for so long was that I felt unworthy and full of doubt. I questioned whether I could truly have a positive impact on readers. I was fearful that my words would not be credible enough to inspire others to improve their lives. And I was worried that my life learning and experiences might be overshadowed by real heroes—like those in the military, public servants such as police and firefighters, and health-care researchers and professionals who continue to search and find treatments and cures that improve and save lives (to name just a few).

Who am I to write a book?

I had to overcome the self-limiting belief that I was not good enough to write a book to benefit others. This is a trait that is deeply ingrained in my DNA. It began at a very early age, as I grew up in a very low-income and dysfunctional household.

But over the years, many people have told me that I have life lessons to share. The first time I heard this was from my future mother-in-law, Jane Kaiser, whose own mother lived across the street from our home in Indiana. She saw the carnage when she visited, but she knew I was very much different from many of my other family members—some of whom would not have been good role models for others. She saw I was determined to make something of myself. I had a great relationship with her and my father-in-law—probably one of the best relationships that a son-in-law could ever have—and I respected her. She was very well educated. One day she said, "You need to get published." I think she saw a kid who had this drive and this mentality to take nothing and turn it into something. "You've got a lot to offer," she told me. I thought about that for years. I'm not talking about a couple of years—I'm talking three decades.

Some people have told me that writing a book would help motivate others to simply become better: to become better at living life, better at managing, and better at being overall leaders. Yet I could not bring myself to begin to write until, one day, the bestselling author and sales coach, Jack Daly, walked up to me immediately after I had made a keynote address to a group of about five hundred people. He said, "Troy, you must write a book and share your experiences with others." Later, a close confidante told me, "My friend, you need to get out of your own way!" He believed that my own limiting beliefs and lack of confidence were blocking my way forward, and he was right.

In my life, I have had the great fortune of receiving guidance from some amazing people. One was my business mentor, the American plastics-manufacturing magnate, Lindsey Hahn. He taught me that business is about putting others' needs ahead of our own and that the quickest way to make a million dollars is to help someone else make their million first. And one of my first military commanders, Major George D. Womack, whom you will read about, taught me more leadership lessons than I can count. My wife, Ann, has been truly steadfast in my journey, providing encouragement and support, building my self-esteem, and helping me to believe in myself. To all these people and to many others who have helped frame my life's viewpoints, I am writing this book because they encouraged me to do so and because I do believe—finally—that I can make a positive difference in people's lives.

My reasoning is simple. I've been fortunate enough to build three professional trade associations comprised of nearly 950 member companies by delivering daily on my commitment to providing invaluable resources, information, and networking connections to our member-company executives. My company, First Resource, exists to relieve the pressure others feel in running a business; my staff members dedicate their lives to helping others live better lives in business. One service I provide includes motivating employees at many of the companies we serve, usually in the form of keynote addresses at company meetings and industry conferences. I have been blessed to receive scores of touching testimonials after these presentations. In December 2017, I spoke at Dymotek, Inc., a plastic-injection-molding company in Ellington, Connecticut. One attendee later wrote:

> I really appreciated your presentation to our employees
> … I struggle as a parent to remember that every day is
> a blessing and not to get caught up in the meaningless
> things. Your talk today has refreshed me into trying harder
> every day, trying in every aspect of my life. Thank you.

My purpose in life and in business is to inspire, inform, motivate, and empower. I wrote this book to help you in your own life journey. When I speak, I often open my presentations with the hope that by sharing my personal struggles and how I overcame them, I might light a candle in the life of at least one person who's present. If I achieve that goal with this book, then all the preparation, sweat, and soul-searching will have been worth it.

CHAPTER ONE

HOW SUCCESSFUL WILL YOUR FUNERAL BE?

Things are a bit fuzzy. As people stare down at me, they have not a clue that I'm staring back.

It's all done ... it's all over ... my time on earth has expired; life's fuel has been emptied out of my tank. The next person in the queue comes up and looks down with empathy in his eyes, but he has a really big smile on his face.

"Damn, Nix," he says with a crackling voice, "you always talked about this time, and now it's here. I remember when I was in a really bad place in my life and was over at your house. You were in the groove, getting all motivational on me, and told me that everything was going to be all right. I was really hurting, and you just took the time to listen, man; you took time to understand; you took time to be empathetic, and it made all the difference in the world. I began practicing focusing on gratitude, as you guided me to do, and it made all the difference. Thanks for being there for me, dude."

A group of three walks up next. They all come together and are at a loss for words. Then one of them breaks the deafening silence.

"He'd do anything to make us laugh. He always wanted everyone to enjoy themselves."

Another guy interrupts, saying, "I remember when I didn't have a job, and Troy told me to come to his house on a Saturday. Three hours later, we had an action plan and began contacting people in his network. Six weeks later, I had a job—he worked relentlessly to get me connected."

As people file through the funeral home and pay their respects, Michael Jackson's "Man in the Mirror" plays in the background.

"I'm gonna make a change. For once in my life. It's gonna feel real good. Gonna make a difference. Gonna make it right ..."

More people file in, and the line starts to grow, eventually leaving the building itself and spilling into the parking lot.

"I'm starting with the man in the mirror. I'm asking him to change his ways."

That's just one of the songs I want played at my funeral; hell, I talked my wife into allowing it to be our wedding song, so why not at my funeral too?

The end goal for my life is to have one big party of a funeral. I'm hoping it's still a long way off, but when that day does come, I hope the parking lot isn't big enough for the attendees. That is the true measure of a person: when you go to their funeral and can't get inside. With any luck, I'll be there looking down as the parking lot begins to fill and the line starts to form. People are having a good time, eating, drinking, and telling stories about how my actions had an impact on them; rock 'n' roll is playing. I want people to get something out of the experience. Even at the point when I am not on the earth, I want people to derive value. I'm looking down and saying, *I did okay. This is my measure of success: having a lasting, eternal impact.*

Of course, I'm sure my loved ones and close friends will be there, along with many of my neighbors and others from my hometown, as well as people I had an impact on in business. But I'm also hoping my UPS guy is there. That's right, my UPS guy, Carmen. He's been delivering my packages for almost twenty years to my office in Indianapolis, but recently I didn't see him for more than two months. When he finally returned, he was bent over sorting through my packages, and when he stood up, I was right in front of him. I took both my hands and gave him this huge shove in his chest. I was like, bam! He fell backward a couple of steps. "Where in the hell you been?" I screamed. "Where have you been, Carmen? I thought you were gone." We had this long conversation. Turns out, he'd just been on another route, but I wanted him to know that I'd noticed and was happy he was back. Wow, just this action in itself made him smile and feel needed and appreciated.

I'll never forget one hot summer day a few years ago. It must have been ninety-eight degrees. I was at Subway and looked across the parking lot, and there he was, sweating his butt off and frantically carrying these packages. When he got back to his truck, I scared the crap of out him because I was sitting in the back with a big fountain drink for him. He said, "Damn, Troy, thanks a lot. I needed that!" Having an impact on others starts with little stuff just like that.

POSITIVE IMPACT

A life of impact starts with self-awareness and looking at yourself honestly. You've got to ask yourself, "Am I doing enough to make the world a better place?" It might be as small a thing as smiling more or just enthusiastically engaging with the people you encounter in your daily life. It's amazing how that little attitude adjustment can prime the pump for a life of even greater impact once you get a taste of how that can positively affect others and how happy it can make you.

And, starting with the end goal in mind—whether it's just a small project or your whole life—is a great way to achieve what you want. Vision and intention are everything when it comes to manifesting something. Vision and intention are what make up the dash—the dash on your tombstone between your birth and death dates. The things that make up that little line are why people bother showing up to pay their respects to your remaining family.

Positively affecting others is so important to me that I dismissed one employee in large part because she wasn't a kind person. She made sure everyone knew she was very religious by always talking about God. She was even in the ministry, yet when my vendors would come in, she would treat them like third-class citizens. Things added up and added up, and then she started treating others in the organization like she treated the vendors, until finally I'd had enough.

I tell my employees, "Hey, these people are important to us, and they're people with their own lives and struggles." For instance, Carmen has an autistic son and will have the responsibility to provide lifelong care. People carry heavy burdens, and if you make the effort to see outside your own bubble, it won't take you long to find somebody who has it worse off than you.

It all comes back to being self-aware. I tell my people, "Lift your head up; look around. When you come into this office, take everybody's temperature, and if you see that somebody is not doing well, then take the time to figure out how you can help them." I have staff right now I'm trying to coach through this because they only see what's immediately around them—their workload. *No, it's much more than that*, especially when you're creating a team. So maybe it's just little examples of giving the UPS guy a Coke. I'm not talking about curing the blind here. I'm just talking about anything and everything you can do in your life, while you're walking down the street even, to do something better. And I'm not perfect at it. I fail more than I succeed, but at least I try to be mindful of it.

FATHERLY ADVICE

A big reason why I'm like that is because of my dad. He was an imperfect man in many ways, but he focused on helping others to lessen their own life's burdens. He was the kind of guy who didn't have any money, and, if he did, he'd often help others with it. He'd give you his last damn dollar. He worked two jobs for the better part of his life and spent many weekends helping people for no money. We would go clean the homes of elderly people or do handiwork for them for free. He refused to take any pay from them. It's just the kind of man he was. I think about those subtle lessons he taught just by walking the talk. I used to hate it when we would get snowstorms. We would have to shovel anybody's sidewalk and driveway in the neighborhood who couldn't do it themselves. Again, we received no money for it, and it was backbreaking work, but that's what was expected. At the time I'd say, "C'mon, Dad. I don't want to do this," but look at me today. Now, I do the same thing, and it drives my family nuts. Needless to say, his funeral was packed. Line out the door!

So, what will your funeral look like? It all starts with a mindset that there's more to life than what's right in front of your eyes. If you wanna make the world a better place, then take a look at yourself and make the change, as Michael Jackson sang so well. You can lead a life full of impact just by taking a good look at the man in the mirror.

LESSONS OF ETERNAL IMPACT

Close your eyes and imagine your funeral. Is the viewing line going out the door? If not, could you do just one thing this week to grow your viewing line by having a positive impact on someone? Could you do just one thing next week to do the same? Do you ever make the effort to do something that is completely selfless? Can you remember the last time you went out of your way to help someone?

After reflecting on this, consider what you can do to achieve your vision of an ideal funeral. What changes can you make in your life to positively affect more people?

CHAPTER TWO

"YOU'RE GOING TO GET PEOPLE KILLED, NIX!": LESSONS ON LEGACY LEADERSHIP

The man who had the most impact on me, perhaps even more than my dad, was Major George D. Womack, my battalion executive officer for the 502nd Military Intelligence Battalion at Fort Hood, Texas, where I was stationed in the late 1980s after graduating from West Point. He was a very important father figure to me, but he was one tough SOB. His end goal was to make me the best military officer possible. I had just been promoted to battalion maintenance officer, which meant I was now responsible for nearly $100 million in US Army assets. It was my job to ensure that my sixty-five soldiers maintained the combat readiness of these military assets, and I will never forget the time Major Womack made a snap inspection one Friday evening. To this day, nearly thirty years later, I still remember the impact he made on my life as a true leader.

It was the middle of summer in the heart of Texas, and we didn't have air-conditioning in the maintenance bays. You're running all over the place all day long at a frantic pace, so you get pretty drained by the end of the day. These motor pools are huge, made up of dozens of giant garages filled with five-ton trucks, Humvees, huge generators, tracked vehicles, and mobile radar stations. We had tons of generators because, when you're in the field, how do you get your radar stations to work? Well, you're not running off the engine; you're pulling around generators of all different sizes. People don't even understand that part of the military. You have to carry your own power with you all the time. We'd work on these things all day long because, when you're engaged in battle-like training exercises, stuff breaks. And to make sure things got fixed in a timely manner, we had to inventory everything from nuts, bolts, and washers to all the commonly used repair parts, as well as all the tools. Can you imagine the number of tools? Some of the wrenches were so big and heavy you could barely lift them.

The motor pool, roughly the size of a football field or two, was located on top of a hill, and my office was in a little shack at the bottom of this big asphalt driveway. It was about 6:00 p.m. and everyone had left, and I was feeling pretty good about how buttoned-up everything was when the phone rang.

"Lieutenant Nix," Major Womack said on the other end of the line. "I'm coming up. Unlock the gate."

I saluted him as he got out of his jeep (yes, we still had jeeps in those days), and he said, "Let's take a walk." We walked up the hill to the motor pool, where we spent the next 120 excruciating minutes examining things that I'd never really known mattered. Major Womack was on the short side, with reddish hair, but he was a stout man who commanded respect with his very presence; he was a true military professional. Still, I was feeling pretty cocky about passing his inspection fairly quickly (so I could then go have a beer with my buddies in Austin) when we came to this row of vehicles, about thirty in all. The lineup looked perfect to me, but Major Womack looked down that line and noticed one vehicle jutting forward about an inch or two. When he pointed it out, all I could think was, *Are you serious? What's the big deal—so it's an inch out of line?* I obviously would never have said this out loud, but for the next twenty minutes, he berated me, up one side and down the other, about my lack of attention to detail while I stood at attention, heels locked and eyes laser forward. It bruised me because I'm a perfectionist, too, and believed my motor pool would kick anybody else's butt. But he kept driving home how my lack of attention to detail could cost soldiers' lives, which I didn't understand at first.

"You're going to get people killed, Nix!" he screamed as he paced back and forth in front of me. "If we tell you that you have to be at this SP"—a starting point on a map or grid—"at a specific time, there's a reason we're telling you that, Lieutenant, because maybe there are things that are happening around you—maybe an assault, maybe close air support, ordnance being dropped or ignited—that if you're not at that SP and you're somewhere other than where you need to be at that point in time, exactly, then maybe, just maybe, one of your troops gets caught by one of those munitions or by friendly fire. Attention to detail, Lieutenant!"

I thought to myself, *Wow, okay. I get it. I get it.* At the ripe old age of twenty-four, I had been comprehensively trained and educated in military-style leadership at the United States Military Academy at West Point. I had been trained in the theory of management, in the theory of motivating soldiers, but nobody had taught me how to run a motor pool, for God's sake. There's theory and then there's true application. Major Womack proved to me that day that I still had a lot to learn. He made a great point, and he did it for a reason, obviously. He was educating me, in his own way, and it wasn't a pleasant experience. He was trying to teach me that attention to detail was the most significant of all activities of a US Army officer. He introduced a lot of stress in my life to make sure that we would be combat ready. I'm surprised he didn't take out a freakin' tire-pressure gauge, now that I think about it.

I never did get to have that beer with my buddies. On Monday morning, I brought in my NCOs (noncommissioned officers) and told them what had happened to me in the motor pool on Friday night. I took that lesson and tried to recommunicate it in my own fashion, which wasn't nearly as harsh. I told them we had to be more in tune with what we did each and every day. Whether it's where we lay the wrenches or how we coach and counsel our people, we need to have attention to detail in everything we do. I was trying to say, "Help me out, fellas, because I'm not going through that again." And I never did.

Whether it's where we lay the wrenches or how we coach and counsel our people, we need to have attention to detail in everything we do.

PRINCIPLES OF LEGACY LEADERSHIP

My men liked and respected me because I was a very humble leader. In fact, I did my best not to call attention to where I graduated and never wore my Academy ring, which some people can see as a pretty big deal. When you graduate from West Point, you're given a ring almost as big as a Super Bowl ring. Don't get me wrong—I was proud of my accomplishment and being part of the Long Gray Line—but some grads wore the crest a little too proudly, if you get what I'm saying. Meanwhile, a new grad would be talking down to a sergeant who'd been in the military for twenty-two years, and this grad hadn't even been in the military for a month. This guy may be saluting you, but you're not going to give him orders. Well, technically, he's got to obey your orders, but in the big scheme of things, he can obey that one and then undermine you everywhere else. It's kind of a cat-and-mouse game, but I knew when I came in that the noncommissioned officers, who had to salute me, had the world of knowledge in their brains, and they could be my own coaches. *They* could become my mentors. I was not a ring knocker. The only time I wore my ring was to formal functions or West Point gatherings, when we wore our dress blues. My NCOs knew that I was looking to them for advice and guidance, but they also knew I had their backs.

I'm sure Major Womack had better things to do, too, on that Friday evening, but he *clearly* chose that day and time for a reason. He was letting me know that there was never a time to ease up on combat readiness, absolutely never a time to let your guard down. Thirty years later as I look back, I realize that he left his legacy on me. He was a leader who led with the end in mind—he was a *legacy leader*.

He taught me to lead by example too. The day after this educational encounter in the motor pool, I was feeling a little demoralized as I was working on my maroon 1985 Buick Regal. Next thing I knew, Major Womack was standing over me asking if I was having problems. He stripped off his BDU (battle dress uniform) coat down to his brown T-shirt and got on his back under the car in this gravel parking lot and showed me how to change the U-joint on my driveshaft. He was on one side of the car, and I was on the other side. Our feet were sticking out, and he began to teach me about how the transmission and the drivetrain work, and I was thinking, *Wow, how does he all know all this?* Leading and teaching: putting my needs in front of his own.

So, once again, build respect as a leader because of your knowledge base, and then be willing to educate somebody like me to say, "Here's what's going on; let's get the parts, and we'll fix this together." And we did. He walked me through the whole thing and ended up with grease all over him. I didn't have money to pay a mechanic. I made something like $18,000 a year as a second lieutenant, so I needed to figure out how to do it myself. Here was a guy who could be such a demanding professional on one hand, yet so compassionate on the other. To this day, when I view him as a leader, he would be one I would be willing to die for. The sad thing is, I never got the chance to tell him how much of an impact he'd had on me. I've tried to locate him but haven't been able to find any trace.

He taught me that leaders always eat last and only when every soldier has been accounted for (especially during a field deployment) and have the food they need. He taught me that the needs of my people come first at any price. He told me that with rank comes an extreme amount of responsibility, and with more rank comes more responsibility. He taught me that you can be demanding yet compassionate. I will never forget when I was called into his office because one of my privates was writing bad checks—not because he was doing it on purpose but simply because he had checks in his checkbook and didn't realize he needed money to back up the paper. Major Womack held me accountable for my private's actions, but he mandated that I handle the counseling session with my soldier with compassion and dignity: to focus on educating this young man, not demeaning him or punishing him.

Legacy leaders work daily to affect the lives of the people they touch—an investment that pays dividends tenfold. If you or those you lead consciously work to leave a positive legacy, then the multiplication factor simply can't be measured. A positive legacy is one where your name is mentioned years after the fact, because you had an impact on the lives of the people around you. If you have an end goal—like Major Womack's aim to make me the best-possible military officer he could, one who would have a significant impact on the soldiers I led, or, in my case, the vision of my own funeral in mind—then it will really help you focus and keep you going when you lose the energy to carry on.

LEGACY LEADERSHIP: AN EXAMPLE

It certainly helped me, after a recent business trip to DC, when I got home at 1:00 a.m. and had to be in the office by 7:30, because we were sending equipment down to Orlando for a big trade show. A small team of seven went down for the weeklong conference. Major Womack taught me that I was going to lead the way in getting this work done, because it wasn't too small of a duty for me. I was not going to sit in my office and answer emails while my people were carrying twelve hundred pounds of material in boxes, trade show booths, you name it, down to the parking lot, shrink-wrapping everything, and then putting it on pallets in ninety-degree heat. These are heavy boxes, and I took almost every load down. I was sweating my butt off, but I was doing what I could to take the bulk of the heavy labor off my people. We worked as a team to get that done. I own the company. I'm the president, and I'm out packing pallets, because it's important to lead by example. There's not a task that's too big or too small, because we're all part of a unit.

After we got everything loaded onto the pallets, I attempted to take a team selfie in front of them, and my

> When people see you working that hard, they want to work harder for you, because they know that you're in it with them; they know you care.

teammates laughed at me because I had to ask, "Can somebody push the button?" To this day, I still can't hold the phone and push the button to take a picture without messing it up, so somebody had to reach up and hit the button. But this was another example of Major Womack's "leaders eat last" philosophy. When people see you working that hard, they want to work harder for you, because they know that you're in it with them; they know you care. You're in the trenches with them. There's no duty or task that is beneath me or anybody else in this organization.

Attention to detail is a critical part of being a good leader, but so is understanding the ramifications of your actions and how they affect others. Even though his method may have seemed harsh, Major Womack tried to show me the thirty-thousand-foot view of things. It takes real compassion to say, "You have to learn, Lieutenant, because your career will be short if you don't learn these things. I'm going to take the time to teach you."

This goes hand in hand with my funeral: What are people going to remember about me? Will they be inspired and motivated to come to the casket and say, "Jeez, I remember when this son of a bitch got three hours' worth of sleep and then came in and moved all those boxes. He didn't have to do any of that. He owned the company, but he did that. He did that to lead by example."

People don't care how much you know until they understand how much you care.

The next day, after shipping all the trade show material, I found a thank-you note on my desk from an employee. "Troy," the note reads, "thanks for being a constant, dependable leader and acting as a great mentor to our team and especially to me. Your passion and dedication are so inspiring. It makes coming in to work each day meaningful. Let's kick ass at the trade show!" That's how you affect people's lives, because people don't care how much you know until they understand how much you care. They know I would do anything I could to support them, either at work or in their personal lives.

That's legacy leadership.

LESSONS OF ETERNAL IMPACT

What are you doing to leave a positive imprint on those you encounter? Do you ever think about or anticipate how you will be remembered by others? Are you building a positive legacy so others will not only endure but thrive because of the impression you've made on them?

CHAPTER THREE

RUNNING FROM FEAR TO SUCCESS

In order to be a good leader and to have the drive that such leadership takes, you need to find your source of motivation. For me, it's fear and never wanting to relive my upbringing, where I yearned for safety and financial security. My childhood in Indiana was a constant state of fear—fear of being poor my whole life, fear my dad was going to die on a regular basis, fear my parents were going to get a divorce, fear my brother was going to freaking shoot me. You read that right: *fear my brother was going to freaking shoot me.* One of my older brothers, whom I shared a bed with growing up, was one of the biggest drug dealers in the Midwest, so we slept with "hardware"— guns—under the mattress. The people who would come in and out of the house on a regular basis were pretty scary. My mom and dad had no idea, and I was sworn to secrecy. Our house used to get broken into, and my parents would wonder, *Why are they targeting our house?* We didn't have anything.

As I look back, I would say we were definitely in the lower income bracket, so it didn't make sense to them. I don't think they really got it. People asked, "Why didn't you ever tell your mom and dad?" Because I was scared, as my brother would routinely threaten me. He took me in a closet one day and showed me a roll of $100 bills that was about four inches in diameter. He then took out a .45, put it to my head, and said, "You tell Mom and Dad, and I'll fucking blow your head off!" He scared the hell out of me.

Although I loved my parents as much as any child does, they were ill equipped to raise an unruly brood of six after marrying young. They were still kids themselves. My dad was the last of ten who had grown up poor in Fort Wayne, Indiana, and his father died of pneumonia when my dad was one. He was a pretty big guy: six feet tall and about 230 pounds. His calves were as big as most people's thighs. He was a really tough man, but he had a big heart, willing to give the shirt off his back to the guy on the street who didn't have anything. As if growing up in a family with no money wasn't difficult enough, he found out he was a diabetic when he was fourteen. He was hanging out with his friends, the story goes, and he chugged a half gallon of chocolate milk and then threw it all up. They made the discovery about his diabetes at the hospital.

My mom had it worse than my dad. Her mother abandoned her at the age of nine; she'd been bluntly asked whom she wanted to live with after her parents' divorce, and she ultimately picked her father. She grew up living in a house that one of my older brothers called an orphanage run by her grandmother on her dad's side. This grandmother greatly disliked and often beat her because of her resemblance to her mom. She used to call my dad her "knight in shining armor," and all I could think of was, *Holy crap, how bad off were you for Dad to be your savior?* It's kind of funny because everyone's name in our family started with a T except my mom's. It was Tom, Terri, Tina, Tim, Todd, and Troy, and then my dad's name was Tom, so my mom, whose name was Barb, was the only one with a B. When we got our first pet, we named him Boss so my mom wouldn't feel left out.

My dad was nineteen and my mom was twenty-one years old when they married and started having kids—five plus a miscarriage in about eight years, and then I came along five years later, in 1964. I don't want to throw my parents under the bus, but they had no business having that many kids. Granted, it wasn't the easiest time to raise kids, either, with the Vietnam War and all that stuff going on in the late '60s and early '70s. And we were all driven, intense, type-A people. Everybody has a dysfunctional family to some degree, but I think my family kind of set the model for dysfunction. With so much infighting in the early years as kids, the extreme differences in personalities and life choices, and with no "mending of the fences," it goes without saying that my family members rarely speak to one another today. It's kind of weird to have a family by blood but not to really be one at all. The only time we'll meet again as a family will be when my mom dies. And that'll probably be the last time we ever get together, quite frankly.

We lived in a small, two-story house with no air-condition-ing, which was common back then. Eight people had to share one bathroom for the longest time. We didn't even have a shower, for crying out loud. It wasn't until I was about nine that my dad built another bathroom in the basement with a shower. My sisters shared one bedroom, while my three brothers and I shared the other, two to a bed. We had two dressers, and that was it—nothing on the walls, really, or any sort of knickknacks like most kids have. I slept with my oldest brother, Tom, and I loved it during the summer, because when Tom would come to bed, he'd turn the fan on us, and the other two brothers couldn't do anything because Tom had the wherewithal to whup them, so I did get the benefit of the fan, which was always nice.

My mom was a traditional housewife who stayed home to raise the kids. She'd wash all our clothes by hand in big wash bins with one of those old-fashioned rollers to wring out the water. My dad worked two jobs most of his life. He worked for GTE, the old phone company, for forty-five years. He had the title of "technician," but he was pretty much a laborer who would repair the switches when customers reported busy signals or troubled calls. He'd do the midnight shift and get off around eight in the morning, and then my uncle Jack would pick him up in the morning, and he would paint all day. He'd get home at five o'clock, and my mom always had dinner on the table. Everyone ate together, so we had kind of a very traditional family in that sense, not like today, where everyone is doing something. We'd all sit around the table and find out about all sorts of things. I'll never forget one night, when I was about eight years old, and I saw this bag of pills fly across the table and hit my older brother in the chest. "What are these?" my mom said. "I found them in your jeans before washing." And my brother, who was about thirteen at the time, said, "I don't know, they're not mine. Somebody must've put them there." That was a constant thing.

My dad would get a few hours of sleep after dinner before doing it all over again, but at times, it was never enough financially. Things got really bad when the telephone company laid him off, and we had to rely on government assistance and food stamps. You can't raise an entire family of eight on a painter's salary, for God's sake. From a security standpoint, I just felt embarrassed to see my mom in line at the grocery store, not using money, and that feeling is forever ingrained in me. Now, while it's true that we didn't have much, I will proudly admit my parents ensured the things we had were kept clean and as nice as possible.

Every spring, to show you my dad's work ethic, all the dressers and the beds came out of every single bedroom, and we would deep clean everything. We'd clean the ceilings and the fixtures, we'd clean the floor and the floorboards, we'd clean the windows and the windowsills. My dad taught me how to take care of and appreciate what you had, because you didn't have the money to replace it. My dad was not a lazy person, that's for sure.

He wasn't very good at managing his diabetes, however. He would often take too much insulin and go crazy because the insulin basically depleted the sugar in his brain if he didn't have enough to eat. He would get pretty violent and wouldn't listen to anybody. When he'd start going down, and we knew he needed something in his body to counteract the insulin, it was like, "Run for the hills," because it's going to get nasty. I'd been chased around the house one too many times, running from him with syringes in hand, but I always managed to escape. Other times, especially at night, he would go into a comatose or convulsive state. I'd see a light come on from under my bedroom door, and then I'd hear my mom running up and down the stairs, trying to get orange juice into my dad. Or sometimes she'd yell, "Troy, I need juice!" and I would just run down to the kitchen, take out a frozen can of juice, open one end, thrust a knife through the lid on the other end, blow like there was no tomorrow to get the frozen concentrate into a pitcher, and hand-squish it into a glass, all in about ten seconds. I'd put about a cup of water in it to where it was almost like a syrup and then run upstairs to try to get it into his throat.

When it was really bad and he would be flopping around in bed, almost like he was having a seizure, my mom would have to call the police for help to give him glucagon shots to counteract the effects of having too much insulin. The cops would undo their holsters and hang them on the door when they came to the house, and each guy—there were usually four of them—would grab a leg or an arm to physically hold him down to give my mom an opportunity to put the syringe in him and not break it off, as he seemed to have superhuman strength when having insulin reactions, and then we would just wait. My mom would sit on the top of the stairs and pray as she rocked back and forth, and I would be in my room on my knees praying that Dad would come out of it, because you never knew. Even to this day, I don't like light coming under the doorway, because when I see light coming under the doorway, it just means really bad things.

The cops were also at our house a lot because of my brother, and they didn't hang up their holsters then. I was always petrified of him. First of all, he was always a physical specimen. By his senior year of high school, he was about six two and 240 pounds. He was chiseled and lifted weights like a madman. He was an amazing football player. And he was absolutely psycho on the football field. He earned a football scholarship to the University of Evansville in southern Indiana, but he only lasted two years because of drugs. Trouble followed him wherever he went. He was half-cocked all the time. I remember one time, my mom and dad actually took a trip somewhere, which is something they never did, because they didn't really have any money to travel. But I remember coming home from school one day when they were gone, and I walked downstairs into the basement, where there were bags of marijuana stacked up against the perimeter of all the walls and weight scales in the middle of the room, along with my brother and two big guys. You know when people say, "If looks could kill," that's the feeling I got when my brother stood up, pointed at me, and said, "Get the fuck out of here!"

My mom and dad just didn't have the tools to deal with my brother. I'll never forget the day my dad drew the proverbial line in the sand. My brother came home late that night, and my father met him at the door. Now, they're both big people, but my dad beat him to a pulp. I remember my brother coming into our room all bloodied up, sitting at the foot of the bed, and then putting on his shoes because he was leaving. My dad came back in and saw what he was doing, and it continued on. My older brother was just so defiant of any authority. And I think it was a last-ditch effort by my father, who wasn't this type of person, to try to straighten him out; I know he feared for his son's future. He didn't know what else to do. What would you do? Your son's using, defying authority, and is one of the largest dealers in the Midwest, for God's sake.

After moving out for good, he got busted with bales of marijuana and other drugs. We're not talking about a little. We're talking about a houseful of drugs; we're talking about a very large and complex operation with other bosses, if you know what I mean. But I'll never forget that night of the fight. My oldest brother, Tom, had moved out by then, so my other older brother and I shared the bed. I lay still as a telephone pole next to him. I heard this noise all night long, and the noise was him spitting. The next morning when the light started coming through the window, I looked up on the ceiling, and it was splattered with blood. Seeing some of this stuff as a small kid was pretty scary for me.

CHOOSING THE RIGHT PATH

So here's the question: Why did I go in the opposite direction? If you have a distribution curve and you put my brother at the left, then I went all the way to the right. I think it had to do with fear of making the wrong choices. Also, my oldest brother, Tom, set a good example for me and always seemed to make good decisions. Seeing some really, really bad stuff actually benefited me. I've never tried an illegal drug. But I will tell you that my brothers did positively motivate me, because they were all very good athletes, and I was too. I wanted to compete with them. If my brother was the only sophomore starting on the varsity football team, well, damn sure, I was going to be, too. So I can't say my brothers didn't have some sort of positive influence on me. Tom, who retired from the fire department after serving for about twenty-five years and now runs his own home-improvement business, would let me work for him during the summers as a roofer so I could have some spending money. He would make me do all the dirty jobs to show what my future could be. I'd be sweating my butt off working as basically the servant for anybody on the job and would carry all the shingles up to the rooftop, fetch tools, and pick up all the garbage, and he'd look at me and say, "This is why you've got to go to school and get an education—so you don't have to do stuff like this for the rest of your life, like me."

I also applied myself academically, because I knew that was the way out of the hellhole that was my childhood. I yearned for safety and financial security. After Tim and Todd left, I had the room all to myself and got a desk with a little lamp on it. I'd come home from football practice, take a fifteen-minute power nap, and study my ass off all night. I wanted to earn a scholarship to college. I wanted to get away and make something of myself, so I studied. I studied and never stopped. I actually got recruited to play football at Columbia University in New York City, and the coach flew me out to visit the school. It was my first time on a plane. I'll never forget the flight and then spending the weekend in New York, but even with financial aid, it would have cost something like $14,000 a year, and this was the early '80s, and I don't think my dad ever made more than $25,000 a year in his life.

Fortunately, I had other people in my corner, like my high school principal, Dan Howe, who told my dad I was "Academy material." He meant West Point, the United States Military Academy. I needed a congressional recommendation, which I got after my dad did some paperwork, and I met with our US Congressman, Dan Coats, who went on to become a US Senator and served as director of national intelligence under President Trump.

The next thing I knew, I was on a ferryboat from New York City traveling up the Hudson to West Point. The first time I saw the Academy was from the ferry. I looked up at these massive gray walls—I'm talking massive, literally hundreds of feet above the river banks—turned to my mom, and fearfully said, "Oh my God, Mom, this place looks like a prison."

LESSONS OF ETERNAL IMPACT

Everyone goes through difficult periods in life. Think back to a time when you struggled, whether it was during your childhood, your early career, or even later in your life. How did you cope during this low period? Have you ever taken time to truly reflect on the difficult times? What lessons did you learn? And how did the experience shape you into the person you are today? Typically, we emerge on the other side of the rough times as stronger and smarter people. The wisdom you accumulate can help others if you take the time to understand and realize what the friction has taught you.

CHAPTER FOUR

NO EXCUSE, SIR!

I was right—West Point *was* just like a prison. And all I could think was, *When is it going to end?* I had no concept of what I was getting myself into, but I knew it wasn't good, judging by the fortress I saw from the ferry. But you know what? I wouldn't trade the experience for anything in the world—it molded me into the man I am today—but I would never want to go through it again.

I arrived at West Point on Thursday, June 30, 1983. The next day we were sitting in Michie Stadium, one of the most beautiful football stadiums in the country, where the Army team plays. It sits on a hill nearly 350 feet above the Hudson River, and during a fall game when all the leaves are changing, you can look across the water and see the rolling hills ablaze with color. It's absolutely gorgeous, but that July first was just filled with misery. It was hot as hell as my parents and I sat in the bleachers on the fifty-yard line. I was wearing shorts, a T-shirt, and running shoes. I had a little travel bag with a couple of pairs of underwear and a toothbrush. The Academy issues you all your clothing, so there's really no need to bring much. The commandant of cadets, General John Moellering, was at a podium on the field addressing the 1,450 new cadets and their families. He talked for forty-five minutes, but I really don't remember anything about his address other than his last few words.

"New cadets, it's time to say goodbye to your families and meet in the tunnels below," he said.

And I just took off. I don't even remember saying goodbye. I instantaneously jumped out of my seat, picked up my bag, ran down the stairs, and was the first one in the tunnel. I never bothered to look back at my parents. As I sit here writing this over thirty-five years later, the emotion of that day is just as strong. I have tears in my eyes because I couldn't wait to leave my childhood and my family behind, and it saddens me that I felt that way.

What do you think was waiting for me in that tunnel? A bunch of angry upperclassmen, that's what. It was almost like they hadn't eaten for months, and we were raw meat entering that tunnel. My new name was "maggot," and I wasn't worthy of being a piece of gum on the bottom of somebody's shoe. Four of them surrounded me screaming in my ear and absolutely bombarding me with insults and instructions. I just remember standing stiff as a board thinking, *What the hell is happening? I don't remember any of this being in the brochure.* They were teaching me four responses to any given scenario. It didn't matter if the damn world was coming to an end; I really only had a total of eight words in my vocabulary now:

"Yes, sir!"

"No, sir!"

"Sir, I do not understand!"

"No excuse, sir!"

There were no excuses for anything. If the commanding officer came in your room and the hospital corners on your roommate's bed didn't meet spec and he asked you why, you couldn't say, "Well, my roommate's the one who made it." The correct answer was, "No excuse, sir!" If, while you were sitting on a log in the forest listening to a Special Forces sergeant teach you about survival tactics as he slammed a rabbit's head against a tree stump, and the soldier next to you fell asleep—which was easy to do because there was no such thing as regular sleep—and you were asked why your buddy was sleeping, the answer was, "No excuse, sir!" I was taught that I was responsible not only for all of my own actions but for those of my buddies as well, and all actions and nonactions had serious ramifications and consequences. If somebody falls asleep, somebody may die.

The second full day at the Academy, General Moellering addressed all 1,450 of us again from the stage in the auditorium. When he walked on stage, we all had to rise and stand at attention. I was sitting near the front, dressed in my new cadet uniform with my hair shaved to the scalp. He welcomed us all (if you could say it was a welcome) and then gave us a very rude awakening about our past success: a benchmark, basically. He wanted us to understand that no matter what we had accomplished in our lives up until this point in time, it didn't matter; actually nothing mattered. You might have been the cream of the crop (which you had to be to get into West Point), but now you were a nobody, an absolute nobody.

"When you hear a characteristic that you meet, I want you to take a seat," he said. "If you're a valedictorian or salutatorian, take your seat."

I heard this big whoosh around me of people taking their seats. I was a bit stunned, because I had studied really hard and had graduated fifth in my class, so I had a great deal of respect for a valedictorian or salutatorian.

"If you achieved fourteen hundred on your SATs, take a seat," he said.

Another whoosh.

"If you were all-state in any sport, take a seat."

Whoosh. With my peripheral vision I could see that there weren't many people left standing. I felt a little embarrassed as I stood there; all I could think of was, *Holy shit. Who am I to be here? These people are amazing, and I'm this hick from Fort Wayne, Indiana. How am I going to make it here?*

What an eye-opening experience that was for me. I just knew that I was going to have to work my ass off to succeed. General Moellering's goal, as I look back now, was to build humility into us and strip us of any egotism we might have had. His technique worked and sent a very loud message to the class of 1987.

"Look to your left and look to your right," he said after everyone was seated. "All these people that feel so accomplished? At the end of forty-seven months, there's a high probability the guy to the left or right of you won't be here."

And you know what? He was pretty damn close, from what I remember, because we started out with around 1,450 new cadets, and we ended with about 950 throwing their hats in the air, so we lost five hundred people. That's an attrition rate of about 35 percent.

My first semester at West Point, I ended up with a 2.5 grade point average, and I graduated high school with an 11.5 average on a 12-point scale. I got one B from my freshman to my senior year in high school, and here I was getting Cs at West Point as a "plebe," as we were called, but it just motivated me to work harder. People would go away on the weekends, and I'd just study. I won't say I was locked in the closet for forty-seven months, but I was as squared away as they come.

Not that it was my goal to be so "STRAC," which is a military term for a well-organized, well-turned-out soldier, but I always made the attempt to follow the rules and put every ounce of effort into doing things to the best of my ability. In reality, I was extremely afraid of getting in trouble or possibly flunking a class, because that would mean forfeiting leave and spending more time on Academy grounds, and I simply didn't want that. I think I had only five demerits in four years, which was absolutely unheard of, and one of the demerits was because my toothbrush bristles were pointed in the wrong direction in the medicine cabinet, which would have been pointed toward the inspecting officer. But that was attention to detail (see Major Womack in chapter two). I ended up making the dean's list four out of the eight semesters. My cumulative grade point average was 3.03, so that's very respectable in terms of where I'd started. So the work paid off, and every semester, I got used to being away from home, I got used to the regimen, I got used to the chores, I got used to the military lifestyle. I started to become comfortable and not be fearful. I started to push some of the ugliness of my upbringing behind me. I started to become a man.

NO-EXCUSE LEADERSHIP

A big part of becoming a man, of course, is personal responsibility, which is a direct extension of your character and integrity. I'm a big believer in the philosophy of "don't complain, don't explain." I admire leaders who say "This is my fault" and leave it at that, even if something wasn't directly their fault. They take the high road. There's no throwing someone under the bus. That's integrity. Becoming a force for good is showing character in all your actions. My employees know I'll do anything for them, and they know I'll tell them the truth. That has an impact on them. And setting that

Becoming a force for good is showing character in all your actions.

example has a constant impact on them. People of character just tend to have a larger impact on society. People can rely on you and depend on you, whether it's your business partners or your employees or the soldier next to you in the woods. They know you're a man of your word.

Ashley, a millennial in my office, is working on getting another college degree, and one of her professors often refers to military leaders. We were in the car traveling to a plastics-manufacturing plant in Ohio when she asked, "What does the military do to create great leaders?" because she knew of my military past. I thought for a second and while I was giving her my answer, I was embarrassed. The question came from out of the blue, and I was not prepared and needed more time to process it. I think at the same time she felt my answer didn't go much below the surface.

Later that night in the hotel room as I was preparing for my next day's meeting, I sat in silence and thought about her question. I thought about my personal indoctrination into the military and then realized what my answer should have been to her. By the time I finished at 0100, I had actually created a full-blown presentation on "no-excuse leadership":

- Excuses won't defeat the enemy.

- Excuses will get your soldiers killed.

- Excuses won't bring your soldiers home safe and unharmed to their families.

The military taught us to be responsible at a very early age. From that first day, from the first five minutes, they laid the foundation of my military career and the lessons that would travel with me for the rest of my life. I was challenged right then and there to say, "Are you man enough to be able to take on the responsibility of somebody else's failure and understand that that failure was ultimately your failure?" If you weren't prepared to do that, then the Academy would weed you out.

If you're leading an organization, the ultimate responsibility for any failure is yours, because you failed to train people properly, because you failed to hire the right person, because you failed to develop a proper strategy, because you failed to develop the right culture, because you failed to engage your people and now they're leaving. It's ultimately your failure, and no excuse can ever absolve you of the responsibility of personal ownership.

EXTREME OWNERSHIP

This was reinforced to me last year when I read a terrific book called *Extreme Ownership* by two Navy SEALs, Jocko Willink and Leif Babin. It's a phenomenal book about leadership, and one chapter covers a friendly-fire incident where one of the alliance soldiers lost his life, while some SEAL team members were injured. They were summoned by their entire chain of command to explain the reason. But in this case "No excuse, sir" would not be a sufficient answer— they needed to find the root cause. This was very serious stuff. They had to identify who had been at fault and why the incident had occurred so they could prevent similar incidents in the future.

The entire company had gathered to debrief the upper chain of command when Willink, one of the team leaders, looked at his troops, some of them still wounded and bandaged, and asked each soldier whose fault it was.

"Sir, it's my fault," one SEAL said. "I failed to have proper radio communications to understand where our positions were."

"Sit down. It wasn't your fault," Willink told him. "Whose fault was it?"

"Sir, it was my fault because I failed to correctly identify the target," another said.

"No, sit down. It wasn't your fault."

After a number of marines claimed it was their fault, Willink looked at his commander and said, "This was my fault, sir. If I had better communicated the plan, this incident would not have happened; if I had placed my troops in better positions, this would not have happened; if we had better rehearsed, this would not have happened." Even though he was not even close to where the incident occurred, Willink was responsible.

Recently, I had Stan McChrystal, retired four-star US Army general best known for his command of Joint Special Operations Command (JSOC), the United States' most advanced fighting force, strongly reiterate the concept of owning your decisions and owning the consequences of your decisions when he spoke at one of my conference events. Former defense secretary Robert Gates described McChrystal as "perhaps the finest warrior and leader of men in combat I ever met." Needless to say, as a 1976 graduate of West Point, I felt like a plebe all over again when I introduced myself before he took center stage; I was standing at attention while I shook his hand. In his remarks, as he explained how US forces were losing initially to the Taliban in the mid-2000s, his words reverberated in me and sent shivers down my spine as he indicated that our "best-trained forces were being beaten," and yet the intelligence community could not figure out how or why. The general spent months and months taking ownership for failed tactics, even though he was, in some cases, hundreds of kilometers away during these conflicts. Ultimately, he and his leadership team cracked the enemy's code, but lessons of extreme ownership were greatly emphasized to my conference attendees of manufacturing-business leaders.

Some of you reading this might question the fact that the military and the civilian world are different, with different motivators. Losing money is a lot different from losing lives. But when it comes to leadership, it does not matter. Some of your issues at your company or place of work might be:

- the need for a better-trained workforce

- high turnover and disengaged employees

- missed deliveries

- poor quality

- lack of customer service

But mark my words, somebody is responsible for these deficiencies and must take ownership!

Just to show how no-excuse leadership is applicable to normal business, several months after reading *Extreme Ownership*, I had a meeting with Keith Shopnick, the general manager of the Indianapolis Marriott Downtown, on a day when Vice President Mike Pence decided to make a surprise visit to a conference as a guest speaker at the hotel. When I arrived to valet my car, I pulled in to a sea of state troopers, SWAT teams in Kevlar, FBI agents, and secret service professionals everywhere.

As I sat in a meeting space with Keith and the entire hotel staff, we began to cover issues I'd had with the hotel six weeks earlier. Midway through the conversation, Keith volunteered to get me a cup of coffee. While he was gone, his staff talked about how well he was leading a multimillion-dollar renovation at the hotel and was taking flak from unhappy customers. "Keith is the first one in line to take any criticism to ensure he protects his staff," said his manager in charge of catering. "Many of the issues are being caused by outside contractors and are out of our control, but Keith never fails to take responsibility for the end results." And compliments on Keith's leadership continued to be voiced until he returned back to the table. Bottom line, they said he took ownership over everything.

While passing me the cup of hot coffee, Keith showed me an award plaque he had recently been given from headquarters for going from last to first in service excellence in the entire Marriott chain. He nodded to his staff and said it was because of all their hard work. Wow, I was impressed—a guy who will take all the crap from customers and not take an ounce of the positive recognition for a job well done. That's a true leadership professional, if you ask me.

After our meeting, Keith walked me to validate my parking ticket so I wouldn't have to pay. I gave my parking stub to a twenty-year-old kid who was flushed in the face and breathing hard, with sweat beading on his forehead. With the added pressure from the secret service and every other law enforcement agency known to humanity, this kid's valet job had escalated to tasks relating to national security. While waiting for my car to be retrieved, Keith and I were talking more about leadership when I noticed the valet attendant circling the drive with a black car. He jumped out, ran over to me, somewhat pleased with his speedy performance, and handed me the keys to the car.

I looked at the keys, at the car, and then at the valet and said, "Sir, that's not my car."

The young man turned as red as a stop sign, particularly because I'd said this without thinking right in front of the boss of his boss of his boss—the big cheese.

"I'd take the car if it was better than mine, but it isn't," I added, trying to lighten the moment up with nervous laughter.

As the attendant left for a second time to retrieve my car, Keith looked me dead in the eye and apologetically said, "Troy, I'm really sorry for this; it's all my fault!" I looked at Keith and said, "Are you kidding me? You had nothing to do with this! Why would you take responsibility for his failure to bring me the right car, for God's sake?"

Keith immediately responded by saying the kid had mistakenly switched the last two numbers of my parking ticket from 0312 to 0321. "I didn't adequately increase the number of staff because of the vice president's visit, so all of the employees are under extreme stress that could've been relieved if I'd just added more people to the current shift. I underestimated how much more effort and stress this was going to cause."

I looked at Keith in literal disbelief. Hell, I thought I took ownership over circumstances, yet he took things to an entirely new level.

It all comes back to willingness to take responsibility. People don't understand how they affect others when they make the decision to take responsibility for any and all actions. We must own what we do, and we have to own what others under our command or influence do, even though it might be kilometers away from us and somebody else is executing the plan. When you get up every morning and look at yourself in the mirror, are you owning what you are doing, or are you making excuses?

When you get up every morning and look at yourself in the mirror, are you owning what you are doing, or are you making excuses?

Taking personal responsibility is hard, but if you truly want a life of significance, then you must take ownership of all your decisions: the good ones and the bad ones. On top of it all, making excuses for poor decisions will lead to dead ends. I've seen time and time again that when people take control of their lives and eliminate the excuses, a life of excellence and fulfillment is the end result. My message to readers is if you don't like where you are in your life and you are looking for excuses, I'd advise you to visit my four responses earlier in this chapter and start looking for ways to get on the right track.

After that day at the Marriott, I thought long and hard about my own level of ownership. I am embarrassed to say that although on the outside it appeared to others that I was good at taking ownership, the situation was much different on the inside; in fact, I was startled and embarrassed to discover that I was really a finger pointer. On the inside, I was playing the blame game.

MANAGING MISTAKES

One of my employees made a mistake while creating a book of manufacturing capabilities we send annually to customers of our industry. This book is a quick-reference guide with tons of information to help land business for our members, and we discovered, after we had distributed it to thousands of professionals across the US, that some of the information pertaining to the capabilities of our members was wrong.

After learning of the mistake, I outwardly was supportive of my staff and of the person responsible for the publication. "Let's just get it fixed," I told them, but after realizing the mistake would cost nearly $10,000 to correct, I inwardly pointed fingers.

Now, this event happened well before my meeting with Keith, but in reflecting on events of the past, I realized that, inside my own head, I was actually good at assigning blame to others. When I realized this and started to examine major mistakes of the past, both in my business and personal life, I uncovered the fact that all the errors, mistakes in judgment, and faulty outcomes of many issues actually could be directly tied to me and my own failed leadership and failed decision-making.

After examining the errors in publishing our capabilities book, I realized that had I been proactive and allowed for a capital investment to make the task of archiving the capabilities and retrieving the information mistake proof, this would had never have happened. The task of creating this book was full of processes that were obsolete; I might as well have given my staff stone tablets, hammers, and chisels, for Pete's sake. The mistake was mine—it was entirely my fault.

I now encourage people to do this exercise in their lives. When mistakes happen, ask yourself the question, "How did my actions or inactions play a part in the failed outcome?" I guarantee that if you do this and are honest with yourself, you will inevitably find a linkage for errors, disappointments, and fiascos directly back to yourself.

The same goes with having an impact on others. There's no excuse not to help someone if you can. About a year and a half ago, I had a man from South Africa named Rae Gold come over to my house to socialize—he was the husband of my wife's friend—and I found out he was unemployed. I was devastated to hear that, so I said, "Rae, why don't you come over this weekend, and let's see if I can help you?" If nothing else, the one thing I have with my company is a network of contacts. He spent three hours in my house that next Saturday, and by the time he left, we had an action plan: one that I took ownership over because I'd given him my word that I would help solve his problem. He was a bit startled because he had been unemployed long enough that people had given up on him. Within six weeks, he had a job with a food-products company. He came over to the house a little while after he started the job and said, "Troy, you don't know what you've done for me." I kind of waved him off because all I'd done was make a few phone calls and send a few emails, and he said, "Troy, you don't understand. Last Monday I went for my US citizenship interview. Do you know the first question that they asked? 'Do you have a job?' Troy, if it weren't for you, I couldn't have answered the first question. I could have been denied my citizenship—something that I've been working on for seven years."

It all comes back to being responsible for your fellow human beings, whether it's your roommate's hospital corners, soldiers under your command, the valet attendant, or an acquaintance without a job. There's no excuse not to look out for them. But you know what? As good as it makes them feel, it makes you feel ten times better. This is where I get my fuel, where I get the fire in my belly. Rae is forever thankful. Every time he sees me, he hugs me and thanks me. I'm like, "Dude, you need to stop thanking me!" But it puts fuel in your tank. I think that's what people are missing in their lives. They have these blinders on and don't realize what they are missing when they opt out, don't think of, make excuses for, or are too afraid to measure the level of impact they are having on others. There is not a single soul reading this who doesn't have the capacity to elevate their ownership and impact over others. If you disagree, then what's your excuse?

No excuses!

LESSONS OF ETERNAL IMPACT

There's an old saying: "Excuses are merely nails used to build a house of failure." Do you ever find yourself making excuses instead of owning your mistakes? Next time you feel the urge to make an excuse, look inward and ask yourself the following questions:

"Who is *really* at fault?"

"Could I have acted differently here?"

"What could I have done to better improve the outcome?"

CHAPTER FIVE

KNOW THYSELF

There once was a soldier in a foreign country who was responsible for guarding a post on the outskirts of his unit's encampment. One day as he was diligently performing his duty, he noticed a figure dressed in black moving toward him on a dirt road. As the person came within range, the young soldier jumped from his hiding place, raised his weapon, and nervously shouted, "Halt! Who are you? Where are you going? What is your purpose?"

The man in black stopped, slowly removed his head cover, showing that he was a man of the cloth, not the opposition, and said confidently, "Soldier, how much do they pay you to do your job?" The soldier replied with reluctance, telling the man of his meager wages. The man of the cloth continued: "I will more than double your pay, soldier, if you stop me every day and ask me these very same questions so that I may someday be able to tell you my answers to your questions."

- Who are you?

- Where are you going?

- What is your purpose?

How many of us have a soldier provoking us to think about life through this lens? Challenging us to find answers to life's really tough questions, pushing us to pause, pushing us to reflect, to examine in order to develop ourselves more thoroughly? This is something Kevin Cashman discusses in his book *Leadership from the Inside Out*. If you decided to stop reading my words right now in order to take action to find your own soldier—the person who would hold you accountable for finding and understanding yourself—then that would be the single-greatest gift you could ever give to yourself. It is through growing self-awareness that we are better able to lead in the most difficult of times. It is through self-awareness that we become sensitive to our strengths and our inherent weaknesses. Although the questions may look simple, most business professionals have trouble providing answers to them. In fact, most professionals understand what they do and how they do it, but few really get the "why." Ordinary people become extraordinary people, and good leaders become great leaders, when they realize that the act of positively influencing—the act of outstanding leadership itself—is not an external event and not something that is simply done but rather is outward behavior that actually rests on the deep foundation of internal values, principles, and life experiences. Taking time to self-discover is one of the most important investments you can make.

Leaders who are driven internally by the purpose that makes them who they are have the greatest lifelong success and the most impact on the lives of the people whom they engage. People don't buy *what* you do; they buy *why* you do it. Returning to my story of my relationship with Carmen, the UPS guy I mentioned at the beginning of the book, he knew the "why" behind my actions. He knew that I was authentic in my pure desire to make his day better; I had no other motives.

FINDING YOUR "WHY"

Very recently, I had a tense situation in my office that left me incredibly fulfilled: my "why," my purpose, was shining like a lighthouse beacon. In a brief and spontaneous engagement between two team members, one senior staff member emotionally stated to a younger and more inexperienced employee that she was not happy with how a task was being completed, and she indicated she would simply do it herself. I took a back seat to what I viewed as a negative confrontation. It was just one of those engagements where I could only express my opinion but not mandate any action, as that is not my leadership style.

In summary, this short but intense engagement left hurt feelings between these two employees and did not advance the company's culture. For the next thirty-plus minutes after everyone had cleared out of the office, I sat motionless in deep thought, working to take ownership of the situation and searching for a course of action. At first, I struggled with the ownership issue because I felt more like a spectator to the event; in the end, however, I'm accountable for everything, so I felt strongly that I needed to have a crucial conversation with my more senior employee to highlight how her emotional reaction to the circumstance had left the more junior person in an uncomfortable state of mind. It was my job to point this out, to educate her on how quickly relationships can be torn down due to faulty communications, to discuss the attributes of legacy leadership, and to uncover the positives of the confrontation, which were not visible at the specific time. Yes, this was my job as a leader, my job to have a positive impact on my more senior employee, because I owed it to her, and I owed it to fulfilling my purpose of having an impact on people.

No sooner had I developed my action plan than my senior staff member entered my office, shut the door, and said, "I'm very sorry for my emotional outburst; I didn't handle that situation well, and I must learn to take emotion out of situations like that if I'm to be a better leader and have a more positive impact on people." I was stunned and full of jubilation. This showed an incredible amount of maturity and displayed a huge amount of self-awareness; I just smiled and expressed my gratitude of the way she was taking ownership. I thought to myself, *Yes, it's working—another step toward building a culture of people first, where caring and relationship building are at the forefront.*

Leaders who successfully recruit and hire people who understand the whys behind what drives them create strong cultures, vibrant futures, and sustainable organizations. Leaders who take the time and effort to find the true meaning behind why they do what they do have the ability to create magnetic and compelling visions that will both excite and stimulate passion inside their employees and create a sense of belonging and well-being. The sense of belonging is what I referred to as camaraderie while I was serving in the US military. For soldiers, this is what our enemies are unable to copy. This is why one good, small team of US soldiers can defeat one hundred foes. We were trained to understand that, when in times of conflict and faced with significant adversity, you simply have to understand that nobody is coming to help, so dependence on one another means you are fighting till the end and will bring the soldier next to you home regardless—that bond is our indistinguishable advantage, because our military has systems for creating it. From a business standpoint, this is what your competitors cannot duplicate; this is what your competition cannot steal, as it is impossible to replicate the true reasons behind why you or your company exists.

Many executives continually struggle to find their competitive advantage; they struggle with differentiating themselves among the sea of look-alike companies, and they struggle with creating a culture that embraces their why. One of the most overlooked reasons for this phenomenon is that executives search endlessly on the outside to find or build their differences when, in fact, the advantages they seek reside on the inside, connecting heart, mind, and soul. If you truly want to become a better leader of people, then seek the answers to what defines the inner you.

Knowing my purpose is what drives me. That knowledge has helped me in the past several years to feel comfortable with what I'm doing, because, frankly, I wasn't always so comfortable with it. I would look in the mirror and think, *Is this it?* I can get in a rabbit hole really quickly when I start comparing myself to some of my Academy classmates and what they've accomplished, from running billion-dollar companies to working for US presidents. All I do is run these little businesses with a small staff of employees, and I can get a little self-denigrating, but I just have to remember that I'm here on this earth to have an impact on others. It truly is what drives me, and then to be able to run a company that exists for the sole purpose of having an impact on executives in business and manufacturing keeps me motivated and excited. I mean, how lucky am I that my life's purpose dovetails identically with my business purpose? People always say that I have all of this energy, but in reality, the energy comes from fulfilling my purpose every day.

IMPACT IN ACTION

Let me give you an example of how my organization can have an impact. Recently, we put on an event in Kentucky for about sixty business professionals. Although the location of the event wasn't easy to get to, people came from across the US—from California, Texas, Wisconsin, Pennsylvania, New York, and several other states. One of my members, Par 4 Plastics, opened up their manufacturing plant so other members could come in and see how they run their business; I call this practice benchmarking. It was a big deal, because there were competitors who came to see how they ran their operations and to examine their equipment and process. It was kind of like if one NFL football team allowed another to come to training camp and watch a practice. The CEO, Tim Capps, willingly opened up his operation and, at the beginning of the tour event, told everyone to do whatever they wanted so they could maximize the value of the event to increase their own personal knowledge, including allowing them to interview employees, take pictures of internal metric boards, and obtain details about how they trained and developed leadership skills. The company and their management team could not have been more transparent, which was beneficial for all the attendees. When you have a chance to experience something like this, you can't help but leave with new ideas and a better understanding of how to improve yourself and your own operation.

This is part of what my team does every day. We get people to share, because we know that everyone becomes better when they openly talk, share ideas, and explore. During these engagements, we usually spend over two hours touring the operations of the host facility, and everybody documents things they see that are really good, areas where they see room for improvement, and areas where they simply do things differently at their company. At the end of the day, my staff consolidates all the feedback and presents it for all to see. My board president, for instance, noticed an issue and provided a solution, and many others in the audience indicated that they had the same issue in their businesses. Everybody walks out better because of the exchange. How cool is that? I was exhausted at the end of it, but on the 350-mile drive back to Indianapolis, I felt incredibly fulfilled. I felt like I had made a difference. My company definitely gives me an opportunity to feel good about what I'm doing. It helps drive me each and every day. I constantly ask my people, "What have we done to impact others?" because I get upset when we get internally focused and we're not reaching out to provide assistance. The more people I help, the better my business is.

The more people I help, the better my business is.

You're probably thinking, "Good for you, Troy. I'm glad you know your purpose, but my job is not about having an impact on people. It's making or selling widgets or performing tasks at the check-in desk or cleaning restrooms. How do I find my 'why'?" Allow me to give you a broader perspective: a personal "why," one that almost everyone shares.

DISCOVER YOUR PERSONAL "WHY"

My personal "why" came from rediscovering my past one Friday night with my wife, Ann, and my daughter Laura. My son had been able to migrate old VCR home movies onto DVDs, so we spent two condensed hours watching decades of our lives develop and evolve. While I was reliving the past, I was totally taken aback. First, in nearly every clip, I looked tired. I forgot how hard it was to be a good parent. I forgot so many things, like those little hugs from the two-, four-, and six-year-olds; the birthdays; the first time without training wheels; and the times at the amusement parks when we could barely afford to put gas in our car or buy tickets to get into the gate.

The issue with watching these videos was that I had simply

forgotten about my own journey—I felt I was in a fog, like that person was not even me. In preparing to write this book, I spent countless hours sitting at my desk, pacing my hallway, and screaming at myself, "Come on, Nix, you can do better!" in order to find the ideas and words to put on paper. Why so much anxiety about this? Why am I sitting here on Saturday morning again, the only car in the parking lot, all the lights off in the building, and alone in a cold dark office?

In looking for the answer to those questions and in being inspired by watching the family videos in my office again, I was completely overcome with emotion—the answer hit me in the face. It was my own personal "why." It was not a new answer. I'd already known it, but it was worth rediscovering—rediscovering where I had come from; rediscovering the people who depended on me; rediscovering the true treasures in my life, whom I had taken for granted; rediscovering my burning desire to leave a larger and more positive impact on others. When was the last time you made the attempt to rediscover your own why?

> **We do what we do—whether you own a company or work in an office, in advertising, or in sales, or whether you empty garbage cans or carry an M16 for a living—because we are working to provide a *better way of life* for someone other than ourselves.**

Let's continue to try to connect the dots. If I asked you why you are in business or why you do what you do in your job, most readers would eventually say to make money, and I do not disagree with that. But if I asked you why it was important to make money, then you would probably wonder on what planet I lived. But really, why is it important to make money? The answer is the same for nearly all of us: We do what we do—whether you own a company or work in an office, in advertising, or in sales, or whether you empty garbage cans or carry an M16 for a living—because we are working to provide a *better way of life for someone other than ourselves.* And the craziest thing is that making a better way of life for someone doesn't even have to be a son, a daughter, a wife, a husband, a mom, a dad, or a friend. If you look around your office or workplace, you might see even more answers. It's the concept behind how US soldiers go to battle. For them, it's about ensuring the soldier to the left and right of them will come home safely. For some readers of this book who have never really thought about your personal why, it might be sitting right in front of you—the ability to make somebody else's life just a little bit better.

MAKING THE CONNECTION

While our personal whys might be the same, we all possess different professional whys, which is what makes our companies unique. This is why my company culture is so much different from your company culture. The guts of my why are very much different from the guts of your why, but when you strengthen your understanding of your professional why, you strengthen your position as a leader, because then you begin to connect the professional with the personal whys. Employees who believe in the professional why of their company are putting faith in the idea that doing so will ultimately enable them to satisfy their personal why. This is where you begin to tap into the hearts, souls, and minds of those on your team, because they know you care about their basic needs, their personal whys.

On the drive back from that plant in Kentucky, I said to one of my employees, "There's a great probability, because you have amazing talent, that another company is going to scoop you up and take you away from our organization, and I totally understand that. I wish nothing but the best for you, but my goal is to make it a little painful for you to consider leaving, so you'll go, 'I don't really want to leave, but I have to leave because I'm going to make more money and ultimately provide a better way of life for the people I care about, but I don't want to leave this culture.'" I want my employees to know that they will never find someone who cares more about them and their families than this organization and me. As long as it's painful for them to leave, I have done my job.

There might be other companies that do exactly what you do with the same type of technology and machines, but what they can't copy are your guts. I live in Indianapolis, home to Eli Lilly, Roche Diagnostics, Rolls-Royce, FedEx, Cummins, and other giants. There are all these amazing companies that I cannot compete with; I can't compete with their salaries; I can't compete with their benefits. But they can't compete with me on my willingness to go above and beyond, to help each and every employee who exists in my organization. My employees know they can pick up the phone at any time and say, "Troy, I need help," and I'll drop anything I'm doing—if they need money, if they need a ride, or if they're having issues at home and just need somebody to talk to, they know I'm there for them. Home-delivered chicken soup to a sick team member or specially made meals to those experiencing personal hardship are commonplace.

That's something that the big companies can't beat. They may win on the material side of things, but they can't copy the guts on the inside. Every leader out there has these guts, but they just have to look in the mirror and say, "What are my guts? What do I believe in? What am I willing to do?" This is why I think my company is doing well. I really do. I believe that. That's what makes it hard for people to leave and gives purpose to my life; it's the fuel.

Who are you?

Where are you going?

What is your purpose?

LESSONS OF ETERNAL IMPACT

Finding and understanding your own sense of purpose can be a difficult task but also an extremely rewarding one. Not only does having a sense of purpose enable one to live a more fulfilling life, but new research conducted by University College London, Princeton University, and Stony Brook University has identified that having a sense of meaning and purpose in life is linked to longer lifespans.[1] To help you find or rediscover your purpose, take time to answer the following:

- How satisfied are you with your life as a whole?

- What is the most rewarding thing you've ever done for someone else, and why was it so rewarding?

- Are you satisfied with the way you've been able to help and assist others?

- Could you do more to leave a larger positive imprint?

If you can't answer, don't stop until you can—you will be a changed person once you discover or begin discovering your own why. This will energize you and give you better direction and focus.

---

1   Andrew Steptoe, Angus Deaton, and Arthur Stone, "Subjective wellbeing, health, and ageing," *The Lancet*, vol. 385, no. 9968, p. 640-648, February 24, 2015.

CHAPTER SIX
THE POWER OF GRATITUDE

At an annual manufacturing conference in 2015, I opened up my keynote speech with a question: "How many people in here are tired? If you're tired, raise your hand." There were probably four to five hundred people in the audience, and at least half raised their hands. That's the society we live in today: people are tired. This begs the question: "How do you overcome being tired and stay motivated to have a significant impact?" Then I proceeded to tell the following story.

Back in the early 2000s, I developed a horrendous case of insomnia that made having an impact on people pretty difficult. For the next thirteen years, I depended on Ativan, an antianxiety drug, to get me to sleep.

It all started in 2003, when I was serving on the board of a health insurance company, the Indiana Construction Industry Trust, known as ICIT, that provided an avenue to offer health insurance benefits to members of my association. About fourteen different construction associations in the state of Indiana had come together, pooled their resources, and started their own insurance company. The insurance company was doing so well, supposedly, that they contacted other associations in 2001, mine included. Some of our members were having trouble getting decent health insurance coverage for their employees, so we joined with the other associations, but I was required to serve on the board. I thought I was doing a good thing, which I was until the insurance company went insolvent, and the state sued us for $17 million.

The problem was that those of us on the board didn't really know how to run a health insurance company, so we relied on the attorneys, the accountants, the CPAs, and the staff of the insurance company to run the business. Basically, the insurance company didn't pay any claims for seven months. I may not have known anything about running an insurance company, but I knew that we were in a heap of trouble. Turns out, a couple of executives were embezzling money, flying down to the Caymans, doing all the things you read about—kind of like the Enron debacle but on a smaller scale.

My association board members kept telling me I didn't have anything to worry about, but they weren't the ones on the hook, trying to run my business, attempting to run the association, doing depositions, and responding to all the legal paperwork without any direct legal representation because we couldn't afford it; I felt like I was on an island all by myself with absolutely no way out. Not to mention the fact that I was directly involved in a situation that was negatively affecting so many people. Can you imagine knowing that regular people were ending up receiving thousands and thousands of dollars of bills from their doctors, hospitals, pharmacies, and other providers for their major surgeries, hospital stays, emergency room visits, and other issues when they thought they had insurance coverage but did not? Do you know how horrible it was to understand that I was associated with something so unethical, something so dishonorable? It was just overwhelming and was a traumatic time of my life. Depression runs in my family, so this just exponentially taxed me. In the end, my association ended up paying a sum of money in a settlement that was covered by our D&O (directors and officers) insurance policy, and the hundreds of insurance agents, and all the other associations, had to do the same.

With the stress of the situation, I started to lose my ability to go to sleep. I remember one three-day stretch—one that is forever imprinted in my brain—while training for a half marathon when I did not sleep for two straight days: Thursday night and Friday night. On the third day, Saturday, I ran ten miles in eighty-degree heat, mowed my lawn, took my kids to the park for a couple of hours, and went to bed at around 10:00 p.m., just praying that I would go to sleep. By this time, my wife had moved out of the bedroom because she didn't want any chance of stirring me in case I did fall asleep, which I didn't. Now it was three days with no sleep. I found myself pacing the floor of my bedroom at 0600 on Sunday morning, thinking of admitting myself to the hospital because I thought I was going crazy and losing my mind. I didn't know what was happening.

To combat my situation, my general practitioner prescribed a drug called Ativan, a benzodiazepine that affects the neurotransmitters in your brain and shuts them off, in order to get me to sleep. But after a while, the sleep droughts would return and worsen even while I was on the drug, so my doctor would simply up the dosage, which only increased my physical dependency. I am embarrassed to say that I was a poor consumer and did not take the time to educate myself on how the drug was affecting my brain.

Fast-forward to November 2014, when I was going through yet another sleep drought. Let me just explain what that's like. It's horrific. You could be exhausted, both mentally and physically exhausted, but you can't get any rest; you can't turn your brain off. It's incredibly frustrating. It's like, *Seriously? Why can't my mind just relax so I can go to sleep?* I just didn't understand it, so I began educating myself on what was going on in my body. I googled "Ativan," and the first site that loaded was for a rehab facility for people just like me. For $25,000, I could check into an institution, and they could help me get off the drug. I discovered that the longest you should take this kind of drug is fourteen weeks, and here I was going on thirteen years. I just thought, *Holy shit!*

What ended up happening is that a team of new doctors created a year-and-a-half-long step-down program for me to rid myself of physical dependency. You can't go cold turkey and simply stop taking the drug because it could result in seizures and even death, but every time I'd do a dosage reduction, I'd go through a week to ten days of these hellacious withdrawal symptoms. The first one is no sleep, followed by the shakes and the sweats, and then this unbelievable nausea and extreme headaches the following morning. I remember one day sitting at my kitchen table and thinking, *How can I go to work and lead my people?* My wife hugged me, and I just buried my head in her arms and started to *bawl* because it just sucked, but there wasn't anything she could do for me. She could be there and pat me on the back, but I had to walk through the tunnel by myself for a year and a half to get out the other end.

Eventually the symptoms would get better, and I'd start to sleep a little bit again for a few weeks, but then guess what? Time for another dosage reduction, and I'd have to go through it all over again—about eight times in all.

FIXING THE PROBLEM

After telling this story, I looked at the audience and said, "So, ladies and gentlemen, do you think there were times during my step-down process when I didn't have the energy, the internal fortitude, to come to work and face my people as a leader? You're damn right there were." I am speaking from experience about how leaders stay motivated, and I shared with them, as I will share with you now, what I did to overcome the challenges I faced, as the tactics I used may be helpful to you when your energy levels are a little low in the tank.

My doctors formed a plan to address three major areas of my life: the physical, the mental, and the purpose of my life. The goal was to prepare my body for the step-down process, which involved reducing my physical and mental stress and heightening the awareness of my life's purpose. These medical professionals wanted me at my tip-top shape in order to combat how my body and mind were going to negatively react to depriving myself of the Ativan.

To address the physical, I completely cleaned up my diet. I only drank water and ate organic foods: no sugar, no alcohol, no caffeine. It was as if I was training for the Olympics. I started exercising like you wouldn't believe and also did massage therapy for relaxation. The physicians also relied on the results of full blood-panel workups to better treat me, and they discovered I had no vitamin D in my system; if you don't know, researchers have linked vitamin D deficiency to less sleep and more disrupted sleep patterns.

To improve the mental stress contributors, they insisted I slow things down and focus on a work-life balance: no more sixteen-hour workdays and answering emails at 10:00 p.m. If you're struggling with having an impact on people in your life, then sometimes you've got to take a step back and say, "What's my speed of life? Am I working myself to death?" You cannot operate in "fight or flight" mode 100 percent of the time (which I was accustomed to doing), or else your body will rebel and shut down. These techniques were designed to calm my body and mind, and they worked.

And then one of my doctors had the foresight of saying, "Hey, Troy, it's now time for you to start focusing on your life's purpose," which was the beginning of trying to find myself. It's why I'm here today, and it's why I'm writing this book. I know it's a cliché, but I think I'm a better person for having gone through all the nasty stuff. Had I not gone through it, I might not have given that presentation, and I wouldn't be writing these words now. I might not understand that I really do live to have an impact on people; I might not have taken time to discover my own "why."

I think it is interesting how extreme personal difficulties often force people to find themselves and their purpose. One outward example is the tragic accident of Matt Hughes, widely considered among the greatest fighters in the history of mixed martial arts, a two-time Ultimate Fighting Champion (UFC) and UFC Hall of Fame inductee. Years after he'd retired from the sport, Matt's wife indicated that he had lost motivation, become depressed, and felt as if he really didn't have a purpose. On June 18, 2017, Matt began the real fight of his life: his pickup truck was struck by a train, and he suffered a diffuse axonal injury, which basically means that his brain shifted and rotated inside his skull, resulting in significant trauma.

After two years of rehabilitation, Matt has regained some of his speech and some of his mobility. But the most substantial change in his life is his way of thinking and understanding his own purpose and the discovery of what love really is. His goal now is to live life and make memories.

To help me find my purpose, my holistic doctor asked me to start meditating on the things in life that are important to me. She also said I had to start giving gratitude by journalizing thankfulness each and every day. The only constraint was that I couldn't journal the same reason for gratitude twice. Try doing that month after month after month and not repeating the same thing. It's pretty freakin' hard, but I started to understand that the more thanks I gave, the more I had to give thanks about. Isn't that a weird concept? Really, the more I gave thanks, the more things I had in my life to give thanks for.

I also started to do research to better understand the science of gratitude. An attitude of gratitude is just simply a good health choice. The positivity creates endorphins, and I really needed those endorphins, because during each step down in my Ativan usage, it felt as if I was living in hell; to think we can generate a more positive outlook by just being thankful and changing our mindset is phenomenal. The problem is that we're sort of programmed to focus on the negative. That's how the human species survived in the wild when we were living in the bush—by being con-

If you take time to self-reflect and show gratitude, it will kick-start any motivational slump you're in. And it doesn't cost a thing.

stantly on high alert—so we've got to fight against that. But if you take time to self-reflect and show gratitude, it will kick-start any motivational slump you're in. And it doesn't cost a thing.

Another big benefit of focusing on all the positives is that you attract more good things into your life because of the power of intention. When you are consciously aware of all your blessings and are grateful for them, you are focusing more clearly on what you really want in your life, and as a result, you attract more of those things. It works. I've lived through it!

GAINING PERSPECTIVE

About six months into my step-down journey, I was still feeling pretty sorry for myself when I went to my friend Steve's house for our monthly poker game. It's amazing what a little perspective can do for you. Nine of us were sitting around the table when Steve came down and took the last seat and began talking about a sciatic nerve issue he was having and that he was having problems going to sleep. In my mind, I was preparing to give him some advice about sleep; after all, I'd become somewhat of a sleep expert by this time. He went on to say a doctor ran some tests and had told him that day, just hours earlier, that he had stage IV lung cancer, meaning it had spread beyond his lungs to other areas of his body. He had a cancerous tumor on his back that was causing the sciatic nerve issue. He was forty-seven years old, had two kids who were just starting high school, a beautiful wife, and a lucrative career in the finance industry, and he was telling us he was going to die.

It was one of the most profound situations I'd ever been in in my life. When he told us that, we all just looked at him and didn't know what to do or say. I was devastated, absolutely devastated. Afterward, I sent him text messages to let him know I was thinking of him. But I once went months without speaking to him because, and I am ashamed to say this, I wanted to avoid him because what do you say to somebody in that situation? What can you truly do for them? I started to feel guilty, so I finally went to see him one Saturday. It was a beautiful early-fall afternoon. It was just me and him. He was lying on the couch, looking extremely bloated from all the chemo and medications. He had actually inscribed biblical sayings on the living room wall because of all the time he spent just staring at it while he was in agony. It was a pretty heavy situation, needless to say, but then he started talking about the things in life that made life worth living. He talked about gratitude at a whole new level, because he was thankful for every day he was able to spend with his kids and wife, whom he loved more than anything. He was thankful for every minute that was available to him; I'm serious when I say "every minute," because he was looking death directly in the eyes.

During our ninety-minute exchange, I laughed and I cried. I was fascinated, and I was amazed. He told me story after story and never stopped talking. Although his body was failing rapidly, his mind and spirit were totally alive. He told me that focusing on being thankful was one thing that got him through very painful days. He also told me giving to others lifted his spirits: things like leaving larger-than-usual tips for servers after eating at restaurants. He told me that the more he gave, the more he had. One story he told that really made me laugh was about Groucho Marx on his deathbed. A friend asked Groucho why he was rifling through the Bible so much. Groucho looked at this friend and said, "I'm looking for loopholes, my friend; I'm looking for loopholes." Steve put on a great Groucho accent when he did this, which made me laugh.

As I started to leave—and I'm nothing if not emotional—I hugged him goodbye and began to cry. He kind of giggled a little bit, grabbed me by the shoulders, slightly pushed me away while holding on, looked me straight in the eye, and said, "Troy, I'm fine. I feel great, and I have to tell you that God has given me the greatest gift. I have lived more in the last seven months than in my forty-eight years combined. God's greatest gift to me has been the gift of cancer."

My friend Steve showed me how gratitude had uplifted his life in the darkest of hours. When we choose to see life through the eyes of gratitude, it changes everything. When we do not give thanks, we soon become ungrateful. When we become ungrateful, we complain, and the negative spiral continues.

Gratitude is an attitude; gratitude is a choice; gratitude is a habit. When we consciously practice being grateful for the people and the situations and the resources around us, we become better leaders; we become better people. We uplift our own spirit, we uplift our own motivation, and we affect and inspire others because of it.

Count your blessings, not your burdens. You'll be much happier that you did.

By the way, as of today, Steve is four years in remission. Since there is no cure for stage IV lung cancer, he is categorized as NED, or no evidence of disease.

LESSONS OF ETERNAL IMPACT

With the pressures of modern-day society, it's often difficult to have enough gas in the tank to address your own problems and challenges, which is why keeping energy levels high is vital to having an impact on others. If you are tired, then chances are you will have little motivation to do anything outside of simply surviving, thereby limiting your impact on others. Taking time to address the following will help energize your attitude and outreach actions:

- How do you feel right now? Are you tired? Really, are you tired?

- If you are tired, and I'm not talking about because you had a bad night's sleep, then identify the things that are sucking your energy.

- List three things you feel fortunate and blessed to have in your life.

- Starting this very evening and for the next seven, journal one item of gratitude before your head hits the pillow.

- What is one act of kindness you could do today that would activate the brain to produce dopamine?

CHAPTER SEVEN
JUST PUSH PLAY

Making an impact in any area of your life—or in someone else's life—requires motivation. But how do you get motivated and stay motivated? The common misconception is that the motivation comes before action, but in truth, it's the other way around: feelings follow behavior. I think this is a vital concept to understand, because it totally eliminates the "I don't have the motivation to do x, y, or z" mindset.

I first stumbled upon this counterintuitive process at a time in my life when I wasn't motivated to do anything. It was before I even began the Ativan-withdrawal process. In fact, I probably couldn't have accomplished that process had I not become aware of the fact that emotions follow action.

It was back in 2011, and I wasn't doing well at all in terms of taking care of myself. I was drinking too much, not eating right, not investing in myself mentally, and continuing to be addicted to Ativan. I wasn't exercising, and I certainly was not sleeping well. I was the heaviest I've been in my entire life. I'm not a small guy. I'm six two, but I was nearly 260 pounds of unhealthy weight. I looked like death. I was a beat-up man, both physically and mentally.

A friend named Bill and I used to meet every six weeks early in the morning at McDonald's. We would try to hold each other accountable in business and in life. We'd come in to these breakfasts and say, "Well, did you do what you said you were going to do?"

But I'll never forget this one day in December 2011. Bill had a litany of issues, like we all do. The work-life balance, or, in this case, the imbalance, was killing him and negatively affecting him on a variety of levels. But when he walked in that morning, he looked completely different and had this "I'm going to beat you today" grin on his face. He looked terrific. I jumped right in and said, "What the hell are you doing?" and he pulled out this book with a yellow cover and a big 1 on it. It was called *The 1% Solution for Work and Life*, by Tom Connellan, and it changed my life.

The whole concept is that if you want to move a mountain, you need to take a shovelful a day, and you'll move the mountain eventually. If you've got a goal, just start doing something. Just do a little bit. It doesn't have to be a lot, but just do something each and every day. Just try to be slightly better than the day before—that's all, only slightly better. I took the book from Bill because I was in a bad place and had to do something. Before that, I was just hoping something would change—just hoping. Bill and the book hit me in the side of the head. You can do something about your situation. Any small act can positively snowball.

It's that simple, and it can apply to any area of your life if you want to have better relationships with your wife, husband, kids, whoever, or you just want to feel better. The list goes on and on and on. Motivation is overhyped. A lot of people are trying to get motivated, or they are waiting to get motivated to change something negative in their lives, when in fact what I realized was that motivation comes after you begin to do something.

ACTION LEADS TO CHANGE

After zipping through the book in a couple of days, I finally started a training program I had been thinking about doing: "P90X," a ninety-day home-fitness regime. I wanted something that I could do in the confines of my home, because I didn't want to go to a gym, which was too much pressure. I had seen P90X on TV, because what are you doing if you're not sleeping? You're watching infomercials. These people looked really fit and healthy. I guess something good can come out of watching infomercials at three o'clock in the morning.

I still remember today putting that first video in and trying to do this sixty-minute aerobic exercise, and it was horrible—freakin' horrible. I thought I was going to die because it was all cardio. You're jumping around and lifting your legs repeatedly up over this three-foot cone as many times as you can in a minute. I was tired after one or two leg lifts. Then you would go to the next exercise, then the next one, and the next one. I hated it. But just starting it was huge. The trainer, Tony Horton, is trying to motivate you, and every time there's a really difficult exercise he would say, "Just do it. Just push play." He also said that at the end of every day's segment. "You can do it: just show up and push play, and you'll see results."

And I did, all ninety days, but I didn't stop there. I just kept doing it—showing up and pushing play—because of this paradigm:

- Action leads to change.

- Change leads to results.

- Results lead to motivation.

- Motivation leads to more action.

- More action leads to more change.

- More change leads to more results.

- And more results lead to greater motivation.

A prime example of this right now is my nineteen-year-old daughter, Laura. She has struggled for years with severe cravings for carbohydrates due to the side effects of a badly needed medication that she must take that has resulted in issues with her weight. Several doctors have told her that if she doesn't lose weight now—right now—she is going to be a diabetic. It runs in the family too: my dad was a diabetic for fifty years, so her situation is somewhat of a double whammy.

She finally attended her first Weight Watchers meeting, and she wasn't the least bit motivated. She was angry that her mom and I made her go. She wanted to kill us because she was the youngest person in the room and had to listen to all of these success stories from people. Remember, when you are trying to affect people and you are standing at the top of the mountain, just remember how insurmountable that climb may look to somebody who hasn't taken their first step. Long story short, she took her first step, and she's now down over fifty pounds and is motivated. The other day she showed me this graph showing where her weight started and where she was now, and it was amazing, and she was extremely proud of her accomplishment thus far. In fact, I think these results have opened her mind, as she is incredibly gifted and is the type of person who can do anything she puts her mind to.

Action leads to change. Change leads to results. Those weight-loss results, which are directly related to how she's monitoring the food she consumes, are now motivating her—turning her lifestyle into a habit—and that motivation is leading to more action, and more action is leading to more change, and that change is having a positive impact on many other areas of her life. It's like a car picking up speed. She's getting more and more motivated, and it all started with the simple act of showing up to that first meeting; she just pushed play!

The same thing happened with me and P90X, of course. By just doing a little bit each day, after eight months I had reduced my body weight by nearly 10 percent. The change was phenomenal. And even though that was a great accomplishment, it was because of all these other things that I never anticipated. I started doing this to get into better health, but I didn't realize that what I was doing at the time was beginning to change the endorphins in my brain. My relationships with my wife and children improved. My weight loss actually became the ancillary result to what I was doing. The thing that I didn't anticipate was that once you start feeling better, the things that matter most to you become clearer. I started sleeping a little bit better. I think it'd have been significantly more difficult for me to get off Ativan had I not lost over twenty-five pounds. I brought in some sort of stabilized health in order to attack what was the toughest thing I had ever done.

BREAKING IT DOWN

I realize, however, that it can be very difficult for people to even do that one little thing to get things going, and the one thing I learned from *The 1% Solution* is that you just have to break things down to the simplest of all tasks, and you have to look at today. You can't look down the road a year, a month, or even a week. You have to take it one day, one hour, one minute, at a time, because if you start thinking about living through all this pain for the next year, it will be overwhelming. When I had my Ativan step-down plan explained to me, it was so over the top. *No way can I live through the next eighteen months*, I thought to myself. But the leader of the medical team of doctors told me to focus on what I had to do today and only today and be grateful for making it one more day into the plan, and that is exactly how I succeeded.

It's the same concept with decluttering your life or cleaning up your garage. Looking at an overstuffed, unorganized garage can be overwhelming, but if you pick up one thing a day, just one thing, and say, "What am I going to do with this? Where am I going to put it? Am I going to get rid of it, give it to the Salvation Army?" If you did that every day, then you will have gotten rid of 365 things by the end of the year.

My son, Daniel, is also using the 1 percent concept to start to turn his life around. He's a twenty-five-year-old jazz saxophonist who graduated from music school in December 2017. His dream is to not only make a living playing but to become a famous jazz musician. I love this kid to death, but I stood by helplessly while he recovered after college graduation from complete burnout and exhaustion from the continuous pressure and workload to meet all the school's graduation requirements. For the first six months after, he lived at home, slept until noon, and then got up and played video games, while I hoped his passion and luster weren't lost. This was not like my kid. My kid is a hard worker. He failed the first time to get into the best music school in the United States, the Indiana University Jacobs School of Music, but he got in on his second attempt, beating out over a hundred other saxophonists in the admissions process. One or two get chosen, and he got selected. It was kind of unbelievable, because he was not trained and had started taking professional saxophone lessons very late in junior high school. At the end of year two in the school's program, he failed his first major upper-divisional playing session—a milestone activity graded by every music-department head—which meant he wasn't advancing fast enough. Add a six-month probationary cycle ending basically with a twenty-minute, career-at-stake, pass-or-fail playing test, he practiced daily until his lips bled. And I'm not just saying that. He actually played each day until his lips bled, for God's sake. He continued to put in the time and passed the performance, so he knew what it took to succeed, but after graduating, he was just spent. I tried to get him motivated and doing something—anything!—but wasn't having much luck until one day he came up to me with a signed apartment lease.

"What are you doing?" I asked him with disbelief in my voice.

"Dad," he said, "I've got to figure this out. I've got to get out of here."

And he did. He had to ask me for money to pay the rent not long afterward, which was an incredibly hard thing for him to do, but moving out forced him to take steps and figure out how he was going to make a living as a musician. He started by teaching students (he obtained a job as a full-time substitute teacher) and started playing gigs wherever he could. In fact, he'd drive two hours just to get on stage for a gig that might pay fifteen dollars, or nothing at all. One night at dinner at a Mexican restaurant, he showed me all the things he was doing on social media and how he was networking, and he indicated that he had landed a gig with Jeff Hamilton—a famous jazz drummer who has been on nearly two hundred recordings with artists such as Natalie Cole, Diana Krall, Barbra Streisand, and Mel Tormé, to name a few—and had started auditioning to play on cruise ships.

"Now you got it, D!" I told him. "Now you're starting to run. You should be so excited, because you're living the dream."

But he just looked at me in disgust.

"I'm not living the dream, Dad," he said. "I can't even afford to put gas in my car."

"No, son, you are. That's what you don't understand, because you don't have the wisdom to understand it right now, but you're truly living the dream. This is part of the process. Do you know how much more fulfilling it's going to be when you're a success because you're scraping by and struggling right now?"

He looked at me like his eyes were bugging out of his head.

"You shouldn't even be able to go to sleep right now; you should be so excited about your future that you don't even want to waste time sleeping," I went on. "Now, here's the thing"—he tends to be a very big procrastinator—"all that time you're lying in that bed, all that time you're wasting on your phone, all that time you're filling your schedule with projects outside of building your business and professional talent, you could be using to invest in yourself. Just do one little bit to land another student or create another social media post or land one more gig, and that could be the ultimate break you need."

I said, "You're running fast, but you're not running fast enough, D. You've got to run, pick up the pace. You may find in ten years that this isn't what you want to do, but give it all you can; just don't do it half-assed. Don't think that you're failing when you aren't even out of the starting gate."

REFUSE TO QUIT

I came across this quote recently from author Napoleon Hill, who wrote one of the bestselling books of all time, *Think and Grow Rich*, in 1937: "Effort only fully releases its reward after a person refuses to quit." Is that freakin' great or what?

If you're alive, you're going to experience the pain of failure, whether it's not being able to pay the rent, having difficulty getting in shape, enduring a shattered relationship, not getting the job you want, or whatever. There's one thing you can always do to make the pain go away—quit, the worst word in the English language. That's what I was trying to tell Daniel after he needed money to pay the rent.

"Thank God you're experiencing the burn. It means you're at least doing something and you're definitely not quitting. You just fell down and had to ask me for money, but now you understand what that burn is like. You don't want to do that anymore, so that just gave you a little motivation to run a little bit harder."

> **We're in such a hurry to get where we're going that we lose the joy in getting there.**

We think we know what the destination is, but it's not about the destination. It's about getting there. We're in such a hurry to get where we're going that we lose the joy in getting there. *Getting there is life.* The journey defines the destination.

The other day I watched a documentary on an NFL player by the name of John Randle. I had no idea who he was. I was exhausted after a long day of work and started channel surfing and came across this unbelievable documentary about Randle, who was a defensive lineman for the Minnesota Vikings. I couldn't believe this guy's life story. He grew up dirt poor in a one-room shack in east-central Texas and thought that somebody who had an outhouse with two toilets was rich because he had an outhouse with one toilet. All three boys slept in the same bed; to take a bath, they stood in a big pot. But they were amazing athletes. His brother Ervin wound up playing linebacker for the Tampa Bay Buccaneers. John played football in high school, then at a community college, before he ended up at Texas A&M-Kingsville (not the famous A&M in College Station).

He didn't get drafted, so he tried out with his brother's team and got cut. Then he tried out for the Vikings, and the defensive line coach said he'd never make it in the NFL at 244 pounds. Randle begged for a chance, so the coach told him to come back in thirty days weighing at least 250, and he'd give him a chance. He wasn't able to gain the weight, so the day before his weigh-in, he went to a hardware store, bought this big old chain, padlocked it around his waist under his sweats, and stepped on the scale, which said 251.

The coach put him on the practice squad for two years, and one day he said to the coach, "My mom told me that if I ask you to make me good, and I did what you told me, that I would play."

"I can make you good, but it's going to take a lot of work," the coach said. "Are you willing to work?"

Randle said he was. "I am not going to stop working until I am the best that I can be."

He was true to his word. Even when he was in the supermarket, he would be practicing his spin technique. It might have looked a little odd working on his moves in the produce section, but that's how dedicated he was. He ended up playing for the Vikings for eleven years, from 1990 to 2000, and another three years for the Seattle Seahawks. Although he was often double-teamed by guys who were three hundred pounds apiece, he became one of the most dominant defensive tackles of his era, leading the league in sacks in 1997. He was so quick and so technically qualified in terms of how he perfected his moves and how strong he was that people just didn't want to play against him, and he was freaking nuts. He stands second in career sacks for a tackle with 137.5, behind only Vikings legend Alan Page. In 2010, he was inducted into the Pro Football Hall of Fame.

I love stories like that. I often use how others persevere in my presentations, because we can learn from them and learn how to get tougher and grittier. I actually shared Randle's story in Milwaukee to an audience of sales professionals from Superior Die—Green Bay Packers territory. Randle was Brett Favre's nemesis. The audience hated him and the Minnesota Vikings, so it got their attention and a good laugh. But something I wanted to stress to this audience was that the "effort only fully releases its reward after a person refuses to quit."

When you put just a little bit of effort into something, it opens up doors of opportunity you never even anticipated. When I put in that first P90X DVD, I just wanted to lose weight and look better, but that's not what it was about at all. What I didn't understand at the time was that my actions to start—to put the DVD in, to take that step—was about so much more; it was about feeling better, having more energy, being happier, having a better outlook on life; it was about improving my impact on others.

And that all came about because that one day, I just decided to push play.

LESSONS OF ETERNAL IMPACT

Have you ever been faced with a seemingly insurmountable task? There just seems to be not enough time in the day, and any action you take feels futile.

I'd like you to sit down and write your end goal. Now write down the smaller steps you need to take to achieve that goal. If you can, keep breaking the goal into smaller and smaller steps. Is there a small thing you can do every day to move the needle? Eventually, those little tasks will add up, and your goal will become a reality.

CHAPTER EIGHT

THE SIX Ps OF SUCCESS

I've attended a lot of trade shows in my life, and one thing I like to do is stay till the very end each day, because you never know what can happen. During one industry-wide show in Orlando in 2012, all the aisles were empty, and the lights had begun to dim on the trade show floor as I started to get my booth in an orderly fashion. I had my back turned to the aisle when I felt this presence of somebody in my booth space. I turned around, and there was this small man, probably about five six, with somewhat of a serious look on his face. His right hand was purposely covering his trade show name badge dangling from a lanyard resting on the front of his chest.

"Do you know who I am?" he asked.

I just stood there dumfounded, because I had no idea who he was.

"No, sir. I don't. I'm sorry, but I don't."

He let his hand drop from over his badge.

"You ought to know who I am, because you've been sending me material for the last eight years," he said, referring to my efforts to recruit him to join the trade association I was running. I asked what the "ID" stood for on his name tag, forgetting it was a state abbreviation, and he said, "It's the state of Idaho, for Pete's sake!" Wow, how stupid could I be; I was already blowing it.

Then he said, "I'll give you thirty seconds to sell me."

I proceeded to just blurt everything out as fast as I could in thirty seconds and told him all the features and benefits of why to get involved with us. Right about the thirty-second mark, he quickly raised his hand up to stop me and loudly said, "Sold!"

I couldn't believe it and started to talk again. I'd gotten about five words out of my mouth when he sharply raised his hand back up again in that stop motion. "What are you supposed to do after you make the sale?" he asked.

"You're supposed to stop talking," I responded, "but I was going to give you a Starbucks gift card and properly welcome you into the organization."

He just chuckled. His name was Dale. He's the owner of several companies on the West Coast and has become a very big supporter of everything we do in the association. For eight years I had been sending him all kinds of marketing materials and emails, and it finally paid off, so I was ready when he asked me to sell him. I was prepared because I've always lived by the six Ps of success: "prior planning prevents piss-poor performance." I tell my people this all the time: in order to sell something, you have to know your prospects inside and out. That's the "prior planning" part. That's Business 101—understanding the demographics of who could potentially buy your products or services.

MY PLANNING HISTORY

Prior planning was built into my personality even before I attended West Point and was a driving factor in getting me the heck out of

Fort Wayne, Indiana. But, not having any resources, not having any connections, and not having any money, I was definitely up against the wall with trying to escape my upbringing. One thing I could control was my preparation. During high school, I used to come home after practice (football, basketball, and baseball), take a power nap, and do my homework all evening so I would be prepared for school the next day.

Of course, the military drilled the six Ps even more deeply into my psyche, and they had an actual name for it. It was about 2:00 a.m. on January 1, 1990. I kissed my wife goodbye and boarded a plane fully combat loaded and left on a three-month mission deployment to Germany. We landed in Cologne Bonn Airport and spent the entire winter in the woods in a war-training exercise that focused on stopping the Russians from invading Europe via the Fulda Gap. I had become a little disillusioned with the army and the lack of leadership (which had culminated in this deployment) and missed my wife, Ann, a great deal.

After returning from this miserable deployment, I decided to leave the military. I first had to resign my commission, however, which was one of the hardest things I've ever had to do. After a lot of thought, I met with my brigade commander to explain to him my final decision. He was obviously not fond of my decision and let me know it. I stood at attention in front of him as he ripped me up one side and down the other for about a half hour, telling me how big of a mistake I was making in leaving. It was weird because I'd just figured I was going to be a lifer. All my classmates thought I was going to be the first guy to put a star on his shoulder, and here I was, leaving. I was the first one out, doing my own thing. This just wasn't for me. Sixty days later, I was a civilian.

Actually, because I never took a vacation ("leave" in military terms), I had two months accrued, so I was technically still in the military until August first. The crazy thing was that two days later, my unit, the legendary Second Armored Division ("Hell on Wheels"), was put on full alert in preparation for deployment for Desert Storm. Most people would say, "Boy, you dodged a bullet there!" But on the contrary, I felt this extreme guilt that I wasn't with my unit and my comrades doing what I had been trained to do for the last seven or eight years. It was pretty difficult for me. Obviously, nobody wants to go to war, but on the flip side of it, I felt horrible that I wasn't there doing what I had been trained to do. I just wrote a hell of a lot of letters to my comrades, because I knew how important letters were at the time for morale. I felt that was the least I could do.

By then I was working as a shift supervisor for the chemical division of Mobil Oil Corporation and working in a huge manufacturing plant making Hefty brand garbage bags in Jacksonville, Illinois, where I was responsible for about sixty people out of the twelve hundred employees at the plant. The plant had several football fields' worth of extruders in a line, pumping out bags. They would run for 364 days straight. They would shut down at Christmas for twenty-four hours and then start right back up. I always thought to myself, *My God, where do all these bags go?* We're talking hundreds of millions of bags.

I'll never forget when the regional director (who had multiple plants under him) would come in, and we'd have about three minutes to give him a report inside this fancy conference room. I would write down every single key performance indicator, from equipment performance to down time to efficiencies to you name it, on three-by-five index cards, because I was scared as hell I would forget something and not be prepared. Everything would be on those cards. I would commit them to memory, and I would practice my "download" in front of a mirror over and over and over until my delivery was flawless.

The preparation paid off, because I was promoted twice—in my three years there. The second time they wanted me to head up a plant's quality system in California, but I turned it down and decided to go in another direction. I wanted to know what else was out there. I was still just a young kid. I'd always had this desire to run my own business, which I was actually doing while working at Mobil. Ann and I were running a small business selling hospital scrubs and medical garments out of our house. There was only one other place in Springfield, Illinois selling them, but the doctors and nurses didn't like the location where they had to get them. We had tubs and tubs of scrubs in our house. I developed an inventory system with this software called Lotus 1-2-3 on one of the first PCs, sold by Gateway before Excel was even developed; it had a 20 KB hard drive, and the only thing that popped up when I started the system for the first time was a c> prompt. Ann would take bags of scrubs and lab coats to the hospital each day, and the bags would always be empty when she returned.

But then we moved back to Indianapolis to be closer to family, because we were about to start one of our own. Ann knew a friend who was dating a man who owned a company called Ray's Trash. I went from working for a Fortune 10 company to wading through garbage in my combat boots and fatigues—they were starting up a recycling center. I hired people who would sort through all the nasty curbside trash to get the aluminum cans, glass bottles, and plastic milk jugs and two-liter bottles. But I didn't like working for this family, because they had no trust in me. They'd brought me in to run the new facility, but I was micromanaged. They opened every piece of mail addressed to me and overruled many of my ideas and decisions because they hadn't come from the family tree. Ninety days into this little venture, after I'd had a major blowout with his brother (who was the president), Mark, one of the owners, walked up to me in the parking lot and said, "You have two choices: you can resign, or you are fired." Nice choice, right? I'll never forget walking back into the house that morning and Ann looking up at me.

"What are you doing home?" she wanted to know.

We had just closed on a house, and she was unemployed at the time. I just looked at her and said, "I don't have a job anymore. I just got fired."

Three days later she told me she was pregnant. I went back to the scrub business full time, but that wasn't really going anywhere in Indianapolis. I would drive forty miles to sell a thirteen-dollar scrub top and was doing all these cold calls. Finally I got one guy, Gerry Gentry, at a hospital forty-five miles south in Martinsville, to let me come in on Saturdays to service his employees. I started doing that every six weeks. I would get a U-Haul truck and load all the inventory on the huge roller racks. I would drive down, sit in his lunchroom for the entire day, and sell $800 or $900 worth of inventory, but it was a death spiral. I'd leave my house at six in the morning and wouldn't get home until eight at night. I'll never forget my dad stopping by one Friday night while I was loading the truck up.

When the doors of life deafeningly slam closed, other doors quietly open, and these doors are doors of future opportunities.

"Troy, what the hell are you doing?" he asked.

"Dad, I'm just trying to make a living," I responded.

At the time I didn't realize it, but that trash company had actually done me a courtesy by giving me a choice. As I look back nearly three decades later, I realize how much of a favor they did by letting me go. Even though I hate to see their orange trucks around the city, I am constantly reminded that through hardship and adversity, opportunities arise. In fact, I tell people all the time you just have to listen; you just have to listen because when the doors of life deafeningly slam closed, other doors quietly open, and these doors are doors of future opportunities.

I was looking for a job at the same time, of course, but I didn't really have much of a network, and a minor recession was going on then, too, in the early '90s. But I kept grinding it out. I had headhunters or job-placement agencies working for me. I knocked on doors and did whatever I could. Every Monday morning—every single workday—I would look out the window and see people go to work, and it crushed me because I had nothing to do. At that time, I defined myself by what I did in my life. It was absolutely horrible not to have a job, which is why today when somebody calls me and says they don't have a job, and they're looking for opportunities, I will do as much as I can to help them, because I will never forget how horrible it was to be unemployed.

During this time period, I obviously needed money. I had to drop my health insurance and paid COBRA for Ann, since she was pregnant. I signed up for state unemployment benefits, because my dad had encouraged me to do so, and I cried in my car afterward in the parking lot because I was so embarrassed that I needed public assistance. It was like I was watching my mom buy groceries when I was a kid with that funny-looking money, and now I was doing the same damn thing: I, too, was living off the government.

One Saturday morning during my time of being unemployed, I was looking for job opportunities in the newspaper and read about continuing education classes being given by Indiana University–Purdue University Indianapolis (IUPUI), which gave me a crazy idea. On that following Monday, I drove down to meet with the director of the program. I didn't have an appointment. I just walked in, waited in the lobby, and bam, there he was standing before me. I asked him if I could offer my own program. Yep, you heard it right: I didn't want to attend a class; I wanted to give a class.

"What do you mean?" he asked.

"I want to offer a team-building class—a class that helps people understand how to effectively build teams and empower people to make decisions," I said.

You see, at Mobil, I had been trained as a facilitator; they'd trained me to build teams. I was one of the few leaders in my organization to have had a department that was run totally by self-directed work teams. I put myself, the highest-ranking member of the department, at the bottom of the ladder and became a servant leader to those who were actually doing the work.

Remember, when the doors of life slam shut, others open. But don't get me wrong: sometimes you have to open them yourself. So I found myself about six weeks later in front of an entire classroom of adults. I had to deliver an eight-hour training program, all by myself. I am not and was not a teacher, and I'd never been trained on how to professionally deliver training, but there I was in the front of the class on a Saturday morning, delivering a course called "Employee Empowerment through Work Teams." It was worth $400 to me: enough to pay my COBRA health insurance bill for the month.

People started walking in about fifteen minutes prior to class, and, with each new arrival, I happily greeted them with a handshake, introduced myself, and repeated their names as many times as possible in my mind before the next person arrived. Imagine this: at the start of class, I had thirty people in front of me whom I've never met in my life. They were sitting in a U-shape format with me in the middle, and I started from the seat nearest me in a counterclockwise fashion, called each person by their first name, and asked for their expectation of the class. I had no clue, no idea whatsoever, of the impression I made in the first twenty minutes of class. People came up to me at break and asked how I'd done that—how I had remembered everybody's name. It was all about preparation ahead of time: I studied the class roster and committed it to memory, of course! The little things make a huge difference.

People enjoyed the class so much that the IUPUI continuing education department put my class in their permanent syllabus. The more I delivered the class, the more opportunities I landed at companies like Methodist Hospital, which began hiring me to deliver classes on-site and had me featured as an expert on team building at their in-house conferences. I know this may not sound like much, but as infrequent as it was, I began to get paid $1,000 for each on-site class and speaking engagement; this was huge, as I had no true income at the time.

A NEW START

Outside of my teaching, on Monday mornings I would put on my best suit and my best tie, and I would drive almost thirty miles to a place called the Business and Professional Exchange, a nonprofit entity where unemployed people could network and share leads. At the beginning of every meeting, everyone had to stand up and do their elevator pitch about their skills and desire. I practiced and practiced and practiced that thirty-second pitch. On my way to each Monday meeting, I would say my thirty-second spiel over and over and over. I was prepared. I talked about my expertise in facilitating groups of people coming together to achieve their best as teams and as individuals. I would also talk about my military experience and what I had accomplished at Mobil and the US Army, and then I'd finish with something like, "My goal is to land an opportunity to affect people and to lead organizations to success," all in roughly thirty seconds—yes, I was and still am a fast talker.

I must have given that spiel over three hundred times before, one day, I felt this tap on my shoulder as I sat back down in my chair. I turned around, and there was a man in a suit and tie. His name was Ed Burns, and he worked for the Indiana Business Modernization and Technology Corporation (BMT). He said they were looking for someone with a plastics-manufacturing background who could facilitate groups. After the interview process, he hired me and told me they wanted me to start a plastics-manufacturing initiative for the state of Indiana.

"We want you to make plastic companies in Indiana more competitive," he said.

But it was up to me to figure out how to do it. February 1994 was the beginning of my new career. (It was one of those really quiet doors that opened when I got fired from Ray's Trash.) I started bringing business executives together at a local hotel for coffee to talk about critical industry issues every month. Six people turned into sixteen people, which turned into twenty-six people, which turned into fifty-six people, which turned into a hundred people. We got so big that I started feeding people lunch and renting ballrooms.

About eighteen months after I'd been working for BMT, around May 1996, a group of these small business champions came up to me one day and said, "We like our direction and everything you're doing for us, Troy, but we want to spin off and make our own organization." When I told the president of BMT, he said, "Troy, that's pure economic development. Make it happen."

That group eventually became the Manufacturers Association for Plastic Processors (or MAPP) in August 1996. I went out and raised $250,000 of seed money from the state and utility companies to get it going, and while I was giving the small business leaders everything they needed to be on their own, they asked me to run the company. I accepted, but two years later we ran out of money because we simply didn't have enough members paying annual dues, so I prepared this enormous presentation and budget forecast for the board. I told them that they needed to get rid of me, because there wasn't enough money to make it through the end of the year. We only had about seventy-five members. We didn't have enough cash flow. I had two employees at the time, full benefits, full salaries, office space. It was one of the hardest things I've ever done, because at that point in time, I had two kids in diapers. I needed the money.

I developed five different courses of action for my presentation; the first four entailed letting me go. I also recommended hiring a company to oversee their operations. The last alternative was for them to allow me to take all the expenses, all the payroll, all the debt on my own shoulders and allow me to form my own management company to do whatever I needed to do to make it work. Get a second job, whatever. They looked at offer number five and said, "Troy, we'll give you all the upside. You go out, and you do whatever you can, but you try to keep this organization going."

And that's what I did. I formed First Resource, my association-management company, in October of 1998, and I did anything and everything I could to make money for almost eight years before the organization really started to take off. But it was hell. Eight years in, Ann and I were still laying out bills on our living room floor, trying to figure out which ones we needed to pay because we didn't have enough money coming in. I'd come home from work at eight or nine o'clock on Friday nights, and all the neighbors would be out drinking beer, having a good time, and I'd just keep working. By 2005, she had had enough.

"What are you doing?" she pleaded with me. "We're dying here. You need to do something."

"Just give me a little bit more time," I begged. "It's all about volume. I'll continue to create valuable programs where people want to join. I just need a little more time."

Sure enough, it all began to change the following year, after my board suggested creating a magazine. We had no money to do it, but we found a way. They planted the seeds for that concept. About three months later, I was at a plastics trade show. It was late in the day, nobody in the aisles, so I just started walking around, introducing myself to people in the booths. The last person I introduced myself to was Jeff Peterson of Peterson Publications.

"What do you do?" I asked him.

"We make magazines for small- to mid-size trade associations."

"You have got to be kidding me," I responded.

No more than six months later, we had our first magazine, all because my board of directors had planted that seed. It was a key moment in turning the organization around, because it made us much more visible in the marketplace. When you talk about marketing, you talk about prospecting, you talk about being visible in a market-place; I lived through it all, and I see the value. I understand it. I can't tell you the number of envelopes I've licked in my life. The number of mailers I've sent out, the number of paper cuts I've had.

The president of the American Mold Builders Association, Mike Armbrust, saw me give a talk at one of my MAPP conferences. Talk about planning. I practice my speeches again and again and again. Not just an hour here or an hour there. For every stage presentation,

I would write out the words: ten, fifteen, twenty pages of words. Because I had no confidence in being in front of people, I'd revert to my old Mobil days with the three-by-five card preparation and memorize all the stinking words, every last one of them. When I walked off the stage, he came up to me and said he wanted me to run their organization, because their executive director had just left. I hadn't known Mike was in the audience, and I hadn't known he was looking for somebody to run his organization, and sure enough, I'd gotten another tap on my shoulder because I'd been prepared.

Just by planning, just by being prepared, I was able to affect even more people with running another association. Same with the rubber-products manufacturers. One owner, Charlie Braun, a Harvard graduate who ran a company called Custom Rubber Corp., heard about me and brought me to Cleveland in 2009 to talk about my method in running associations, because his industry sector needed one. During this discussion, I found out I was up against some large management companies that were running over one hundred associations. Charlie called me soon afterward and said he and the rubber-industry steering team wanted to do a "site visit." At the time I had two employees and a seven-hundred-square-foot office.

"Charlie," I said, "I don't have anything to show you here."

"Doesn't matter," he shot back. "We want to come out and visit you."

I brought Ann in so it would look like we had a larger staff. Charlie walked in with two other company owners, but instead of me selling them on why they should hire me, I put together a series of meetings outside my business space, because I didn't want my office to leave a negative impression and to affect them in terms of how they looked at me. I took them to the presidents of some of the companies that belonged to the organizations I was running, like Lindsey Hahn of Metro Plastics, my mentor, who was my first volunteer president.

"I'm not going to sell you on my running your organization," I told Charlie and the others. "I'm going to let my customers do it."

They spent the whole day interviewing people I worked for. Two or three weeks later, Charlie called me while I was watching my son run a track meet.

"Troy, I have good news and bad news," he said. "The good news is that we've selected you to develop and incorporate and create a rubber-processors organization. The bad news is we have no money to pay you for the first year."

"Charlie, what's the bad news?" I asked him, and he repeated it, wondering why I was so agreeable. "I used to sleep in the back of my car selling memberships for my first trade association, MAPP. Nothing comes easy in this life. We'll make this into something, and then, when you have enough money, then you can pay me."

Today, that group has more than two hundred different facility locations in the organization, and it represents about a quarter of our revenue, all because of my preparation and plan to have my customers sell them. I could have sat in my office and done my best to gloat, but I don't toot my own horn very well, so I let my customers gloat for me. My office has grown to ten people and has tripled in size, with a kitchen and conference room—still very modest, but beautiful to me, because it allows me to better affect the people who are members in the associations we run.

Life is better now; Ann does not have to lay the bills on the living room floor to figure out how we are going to pay them, and that feels good. I've got a great organization, and my team runs many different associations. On top of that, I am a motivational speaker and travel around the world inspiring others to believe they can leave a larger positive footprint on the life they lead. So it's all come to fruition, but if I didn't get up that one day at the Business and Professional Exchange and do my act perfectly in that thirty seconds, then maybe I never would have gotten a tap on my shoulder, and who knows where I would be today?

Prior planning. My slogan when I was younger was that it seemed the harder I worked, the luckier I became. As I look back, I did what I could with the six Ps and eliminated luck altogether.

LESSONS OF ETERNAL IMPACT

Thinking about your own life and work, are you doing what you need to do to be prepared?

Think of the doors that have loudly closed on you over your lifetime. Can you identify the ones that silently opened for you? As we continue to experience failure, understanding this concept can help in the tough times.

CHAPTER NINE
THE POWER OF PERSEVERANCE

In 1953, three employees of the Rocket Chemical Company set out to create a rust-prevention solvent for use in the aerospace industry; the solvent was first used as a protection element on the outer skin of Atlas rockets, the United States' first operational intercontinental ballistic missiles. The product inventors tried not once, not twice, not three times. They tried forty times before they finally created the product that virtually everyone in America has used at one time or another since then: WD-40, or "Water Displacement, 40th Formula."

How many of you reading this book have failed at anything thirty-nine times, only to try a fortieth time to succeed? Now, that's perseverance: the act of doing something despite the difficulties in order to achieve a goal or to become victorious. We all do it to one degree or another. Most successful people are standing atop a mountain of failure.

Most successful people are standing atop a mountain of failure.

There is not a lot of science behind what creates perseverance in a person, but I was enamored by research conducted by Angela Lee Duckworth, a professor of psychology at the University of Pennsylvania who led an intensive study about factors that make people successful.[2] (Her 2013 TED Talk on her findings has had more than sixteen million views.) She and her team studied the performance of people in a variety of organizations and situations and tried to predict who would succeed and who would fail. They examined the National Spelling Bee competition and tried to predict who would advance the farthest. They also studied the new cadet class at West Point and tried to predict who would stay and graduate, which I found particularly interesting, since so many left during my four-year process. They studied rookie teachers in tough neighborhoods and set up models to forecast who would last the longest and be the most successful in producing the best outcomes. They studied salespeople in private business and attempted to calculate who would be the best salesperson, make the most money, and bank the greatest commission dollars.

At the conclusion of the research, in all cases, one characteristic emerged as the predictor of success: it was not IQ, as I had originally thought; it was not social intelligence, not good looks, nor good social status. The one characteristic was grit—a passion and perseverance for very long-term goals. Grit means having stamina and sticking with your future day in, day out, relentlessly, because of the vision of what's at the end of the journey. Science tells us that one thing is for certain about grit: there is a mindset associated with grittiness, and your mindset changes and grows by being challenged. As a result, those who consistently challenge themselves seem much more likely to persevere when they fail because they don't believe that failure is a permanent condition. Grit is a mindset. It's as if the mind is a muscle that can change over time if you continue to step out of the box and are okay with being uncomfortable. The more failure you're bombarded with, the less failure will have an impact on your

2   Angela Duckworth, accessed October 2, 2019, http://angeladuckworth.com/.

outlook of the long-term goal, because failure is only temporary.

Grit is a strong vision of the future, much like when Olympic athletes picture a perfect routine or perfect race that they play time and time again in their mind until they actually are able to perform it. The body follows the mind, which is how I got through West Point. The only thing that prevented me from jumping out the window, the only thing that prevented me from leaving, was seeing myself on the fifty-yard line throwing my hat in the air on graduation day. I envisioned that day on every single one of the nearly 1,410 days I was on Academy grounds: forty-seven months of training and education. I counted the days, and I continued to see myself throwing my hat in the air. Having that end goal in mind was incredibly powerful and acted like a magnet to my future.

One way you can enhance your own level of perseverance is by understanding how others have survived really tough times, like my friend and fellow author and speaker Alan Hobson. Alan is a former nine-time all-American gymnast who summited Mount Everest on his third self-guided and self-organized expedition. It took him ten years—an act of extreme persistence. Three years after standing on top of the world, however, he found himself at the bottom when he was diagnosed with a very aggressive blood cancer called acute myeloid leukemia. At diagnosis, 90 percent of the cells in his bone marrow were cancerous. Without treatment, he was told he would have less than a year to live. Even if he did, the three-year survival rate was 15 percent or less—to say nothing of the quality of life he might have if he did survive.

He told me that, when he was on the cancer ward, one of the tools he used to help get him through over five hundred hours of chemotherapy and an adult blood stem cell transplant (the modern-day equivalent of a bone marrow transplant) was a picture of a sweeping mountain scene he had on the wall of his hospital room. Every day, several times a day, he would look at it and imagine himself standing in that scene. He imagined what it would look like, feel like, and sound like, even what it would smell like as the scent of pine and spruce wafted through his nostrils. He was determined to do everything in his power to maximize his chances of surviving to walk straight into that scene.

In addition to outstanding medical care and the solid support of family and friends, one of the things that helped him climb his "inner Everest" was the power of this persistent vision. Whenever he found himself falling into fear, he returned to that scene in his mind, over and over again. That, combined with daily meditation, a balanced diet, lots of water, proper rest, a focus on healing rather than dying, and regular cardiovascular activity eventually enabled him to make a 100 percent recovery.

Three years after his treatment ended, he was on a hike in the mountains. He looked up and suddenly realized that the scene he had imagined hundreds of times in his mind had materialized before his very eyes. He not only survived to thrive beyond cancer that time, but he did it again when he was diagnosed with a different form of the disease ten years later. He is now officially medically cured. His is a true tale of persistence and tenacity. I highly recommend reading the book *Climb Back from Cancer* (coauthored with Cecilia Hobson) and subscribing to his innovative online offering, the Climb Back from Cancer Survivorship Program, if you know anyone who has just been diagnosed.[3]

The one major thing that I've learned about perseverance is that we can all become mentally tougher. In the end, the only thing that

---

3   The Climb Back from Cancer Survivorship Program, accessed October 2, 2019, https://survivecancer.ca.

makes a person give up and quit are the thoughts that drive the final behavior; it's all about mental fatigue. I think David Goggins, the only member of the US armed forces to complete SEAL training (including two hell weeks), the US Army Ranger School (where he graduated as "enlisted honor man"), Air Force Tactical Air Controller training, and world-class endurance athlete, has summed it up the best. I must say that I respect the hell out of this man's accomplishments. He's faced adversity his entire life and has successfully overcome a hell of a lot of pain and hardship. He said in a YouTube interview that "your mind has a tactical advantage over you, as it knows your fears and your insecurities; it knows where you don't want to go, so it will guide you away" to keep you safe. In the end, your mind always wins, so his staunch advice is to reprogram your mind by doing things that make you uncomfortable and put you well outside your zone. As David puts it, there is only one way to build mental toughness, and that is to "do things you don't like to do" and to do those things often. If you have control over your mind and your mind has ultimate control over you, then reprogramming makes perfect sense, doesn't it?

MY RESPONSIBILITY

Here's one way I became a little grittier and hard-nosed. In 2016, I had to participate in a service that involved laying my father-in-law, Bob, to his final resting place. He had been in my life for thirty-six years. He was actually in my life longer than my own dad was, so we'd had a special relationship. He was a cool man. The relationship that he had with our kids was phenomenal. If you painted a picture of a perfect grandfather, it would've been him. He didn't have a judging bone in his body. He just simply loved. What an example he set for me. As you can imagine, this day was extremely difficult for me, my wife, and our kids. The unexpected thing, however, was the fact that this day actually turned into a celebration, and it affected the way I view my own life challenges and actually fueled me. Some of the context that follows is wrapped in a religious context, but in no way is it my intention to deliver a religious message.

The agenda for the day was to have a two-hour wake, followed by a small ceremony. At a couple of minutes before the end of the wake, a clergyman walked in and took position at the front of the room, silently standing halfway between my father-in-law's casket and the front row of about eight folding chairs. He was dressed all in black and had perfectly combed jet-black hair. Although he was on the short side, he had this imposing stature. Without him saying a word, those in the room felt his presence and took their seats. At exactly 4:00 p.m., the preacher got up and took his place behind a podium. He opened up the Good Book and began reading verses of scripture. I've listened to church sermons once a week for the better part of my life. I've attended lectures by accomplished PhD professors and have participated in many business conferences with in-demand speakers, but I have never, I repeat never, been affected by someone more than this preacher affected me. His oration skills were mesmerizing, even though he never once looked up. *He became the scripture.* He read the passages as if he'd actually written them, and for some reason, they had extensive meaning to me then, more than at any other time in my life.

He selected verses that showcased how death could be a robber in the night, how death could cheat us, how death could sting if we allowed it to. When he was finished, he slowly put the good book in the upper-right-hand corner of the podium and moved in front of it. This was the first time he set eyes on us. Patiently, almost ensuring that he'd make eye contact with everyone in the audience before proceeding, he then bellowed, "When a bad man dies, the world rejoices! When a good man dies, you can hear a pin drop."

His voice cut to my core, and his tone made the hair on the back of my neck stand at rigid attention. His stare was intense and stern; he was almost angry. He then proceeded to talk about Bob as a good man but a common man who never made the newspaper or the nightly news or won any awards. He was never employee of the month or received any other accolades of accomplishment. He recited a pretty exhaustive list of what had made Bob a common man, which made everyone in the room feel pretty common too. I know I did. But that's when he pulled the old bait and switch, when he demonstrated how this simple common man had affected hundreds and hundreds of people, some of whom were sitting in the audience but most of whom would remain nameless and faceless throughout his life through his unselfish service and stewardship. He talked about how Bob had positively affected soldiers while serving in the Korean War. He spoke of Bob's nearly sixty-year marriage to his wife, Jane; how he gave every ounce of energy to raising his two adopted kids, Bill and Ann; and how he'd left an imprint on the entire neighborhood and community. He talked about how he'd touched the lives of nearly every resident in the nursing home where he'd spent his last years.

But what got me more than anything was when he started talking about Bob as an artist. He would go through the retirement facility with his iPad—he loved gadgets—and would take pictures of people. He would then print out the photos and make kites out of them with bamboo sticks and rice paper, and he'd go outside in the parking lot and fly them with the person. Other residents would come out, too, and they would laugh and point. "Look at Mary in the sky!"

They would even get in trouble, because they weren't supposed to be outside of the facility, but he really brought a few moments of joy to the otherwise depressing situation of being in a nursing home.

The preacher stopped as suddenly as he'd begun and looked the room over. It was a bit eerie the way he seemed to silently connect with everyone there.

"Do not let death win," he said loudly. "Each of you has a responsibility not to let it win. And you will succeed as long as you remember Bob's virtues and work to be curious, work to continually learn, work to live each day to its fullest, and work to be young and kidlike." At one point, the preacher screamed, "Shame on you if you are forty years old and not reading books and working to better yourself, because that's what Bob would have wanted!" And screamed again, "Shame on you if you do not give gratitude and work to cherish every moment on this earth, as this is what Bob would have wanted!"

It was an amazing sermon, one that stayed with me for weeks afterward, especially when it came to persevering through tough times. As a common man, I now know that I affect people in more ways than I understand and that most of those people will remain nameless and faceless until the day I die. So I have a responsibility to pick myself up in times of adversity, because people depend on me to do so. I have a responsibility to work harder when things don't go my way and to shift focus from self to focus on others during extreme times. I have a responsibility to dedicate my talents and my intellect to find new methods and innovations at work, because the organizations we serve depend on that. I have a responsibility to remain steadfast in my own life, as this is what Bob would have wanted.

PUSHING THROUGH

As I look back on my life, I realize that tough experiences have helped to fortify my brain and my brain's thought processes. The more times you put yourself out there in tough situations and fail, the more failure just doesn't matter, just like Dr. Duckworth has explained. And we learn from failure.

I failed the other day—I failed miserably the other day—but the learning on the other side of my failure was incredibly immense. I'd signed up for an athletic challenge because of the encouragement of my daughter, Maria. The challenge: do a two-thousand-meter row, three hundred body-weight exercises (one hundred squats, eighty bench step-ups, forty burpees, forty pushups, and forty plank jacks), and a 3.1-mile run as fast as I could. Obviously, before the competition I'd set a goal, I had a strategy, and I'd been training for months. I asked an audience the other day, as I showed them the end results of my heart rate graph during the competition, gathered from my monitor, "At what point during the competition did I feel the most confident and comfortable? And at what point did I feel the most uncomfortable and lack the most confidence?"

The audience picked the times where my heart rate was the lowest and logically said that that was when I'd felt the most confident, and where my heart rate was the highest, that was where I was the most uncomfortable. They were logical in their thinking, but they were dead wrong. The segments of the competition when my heart rate was the lowest was when I'd begun to give up: when I'd started to pull the throttle back because I was talking myself into the fact that I could not meet my goal. I was not good enough or in shape enough to handle the challenge.

"What in the hell am I doing here?" I said. "This is too damn painful!"

The pain was the worst I'd felt in over three decades since leaving the military; it was all out for nearly fifty minutes, and halfway through, I was listening to that little negative voice in my head to quit and was 100 percent focused on the pain and nothing else. Roughly two-thirds through the entire event and a third of the way through my 5K run, I began to walk, and it was at this point that I saw the first person actually finish the competition: a bald guy who I thought was close to my age. I immediately began to self-reflect, and that self-reflection turned the tide.

"Why am I focusing on the pain?"

"Why am I telling myself I can't finish?"

"Why am I convincing myself that I'm going to fail?"

It was at this point that I switched my thinking. I began to focus on all the good things. I began to tell myself that I'd felt the same level of pain in the past, and I began to coach myself as to how well I was actually doing. At the time when my heart rate was the highest, I was running my fastest and felt my best, and that was at the tail end of the competition, around forty-seven minutes deep. It's funny how the mind works. As the famous life coach and author Tony Robbins explains, "Confidence is not something you have; it is something that you create."

Everyone has the power to instantaneously think differently, but to conquer this feat you have to be self-aware. I finished the competition and failed to meet my goal, but it didn't matter; I learned a tremendous amount and will beat an even faster goal time at the next event. I'm a veteran now, and I'm doing it again because I love the pain and know that my failure to meet my goal was only a temporary setback.

LESSONS OF ETERNAL IMPACT

When you are in tough places in your life and in your business, when you feel down and as if you cannot go on, summon energy and excitement from knowing you have to carry the load to enable others to succeed along with you. Do not let them down, as you know that your own impact will be much greater than the task at hand and that this impact will be felt by people far beyond your own level of understanding.

CONCLUSION

About three weeks after Bob's funeral, our family took a trip to Mexico to help us recover from his passing, and one of my friends who sits on my board of directors had some advice for me.

"Troy, do me a favor," he said. "Read a novel or something. Quit reading all those self-help books."

I laughed and said okay. The book I brought along on the trip was one a neighbor had given me a few years earlier called *Bobblehead Dad*, by Jim Higley. Turns out it wasn't a novel, but at least it wasn't a self-help book, either, at least not overtly. The title refers to how Jim had gone through life like one of those collectible figurines with the springy head, just bouncing along until he was stricken with cancer at the age of forty after losing his grandmother, mom, and other family members to the disease. One day, he ran into a friend of a friend who was a cancer survivor, so they decided to grab a cup of coffee together.

"Jim, you're going to receive the most amazing gifts as you go through this," she promised. "You may not even realize it at the time, but if your mind and heart are open, I promise you will come out of this with a gift that will change your life. Your gift will be yours and yours alone. And you will never be the same. Regardless of what happens with your cancer."

A gift for me? What? Jim was a little perplexed, because he couldn't see the gifts yet. The reader can, but he couldn't until one day he found a treasure chest in the attic that contained his late mother's purse. Now, as he looked back, he'd never been able to truly understand how his mother had so positively dealt with her situation with cancer in the midst of all the agony; she'd always had a smile on her face, was always helping others, and was intent on making the lives of other people just a little bit better.

He opened the purse and discovered a piece of paper with the "Salesman's Prayer" by Heartsill Wilson written on it:

This is the beginning of a new day.
God has given me this day to use as I will.
I can waste it or use it for good.
What I do today is important because I am exchanging a day of my life for it.
When tomorrow comes, this day will be gone forever, leaving in its place something I have traded for it.
I want it to be a gain, not a loss—good not evil.
Success, not failure, in order that I shall not regret the price I paid for it.

Finally, he discovered his gift. Reading those words on the back of that little piece of paper helped him to realize that this was how his mother had lived. She cherished the moments in other people's lives and understood that those moments and every story all contained potential lessons. "If you miss a 'today,' you miss all of its lessons. That's why it's important to live in the moment."

This image of a quarter-full gas tank represents what I have left of my life. The average American male lives to be 76.1 years old. I'm fifty-five years old, so that means I have a little bit above a quarter-tank left. Where is the needle in your life? Unfortunately, unlike with a real gas tank, there is no gas station on this earth where you can go and put an extra minute in the tank. There's nowhere to refill it. You are done when it's done, and that's if everything goes well with your remaining time. After I said this to a group of business executives, an older man pulled me aside and said, "Troy, what happens in your car when you get to an eighth of a tank?" I took a step back and was caught off guard by my own analogy. He told me that "it goes down pretty quick from there!" So, I actually have less than a quarter of a tank.

When you're struggling, when you're in life's troughs, you had better put 110 percent of your effort into getting out of that downside, because you don't have a lot of time. You have to do anything you can to get out of the trough, because the seconds are ticking.

One of the things Jim Higley used to do before his cancer diagnosis was to live for his weekends. I'm sure a lot of you reading this do that too, but if you do, that means you're throwing away about 70 percent of your life each week. You are wasting valuable fuel. Every day. After surviving his cancer, Jim started looking at life a little differently and now had a great deal of gratitude for being able to go to work because he was no longer in pain. The key is to see the gifts in your life without having to get cancer first. I do not let my children leave the house until I hug the crap out of them and tell them I love them, because they are precious gifts.

My hope is that this book provides a guiding light for you as you implement positive-impact leadership in your own work and life. I hope your funeral is packed full of family and friends and others you have influenced and positively touched along the way. I hope there's not enough room for all the attendees who want to honor your deeds. I think if we can all live our lives like that, then the world will be a far better place.

Most of our daily experiences come and go and really never register with us. They all seem to be very mundane things that never amount to anything, but all moments matter, because you have the chance to make a difference in someone's life each and every day. Most of the things that shape our day-to-day lives come from simple and seemingly insignificant moments throughout our lives. The sooner you realize that, the sooner you can take the time to study the "Man in the Mirror" and understand, and then the sooner the new and improved, happier and grittier you will have a greater, more positive impact on people, both in business and in life—many of whom will remain nameless and faceless until the day you die!

ABOUT THE AUTHOR

Troy Nix is a business leader, international motivational speaker, father, and friend to many who has spent nearly three decades positively influencing people.

Troy graduated from the United States Military Academy at West Point in 1987, where he received a bachelor of science in engineering management. He became a trained military parachutist, qualified to participate in airborne operations, in 1986 and went on to serve as an ordnance officer in the US Army with both the 502nd Military Intelligence Battalion and the 2nd Armored Division. After leaving the military, Troy joined the operations of Mobil Chemical Company where he was introduced to high-speed manufacturing that would form the foundation for his manufacturing services company.

Troy currently serves as the founder, president, and CEO of First Resource, Inc. the only association management company focused exclusively on providing value to America's manufacturers through innovative association management practices. A thirty-year veteran of the manufacturing sector, Troy serves as the founding executive director of the Manufacturers Association for Plastics Processors (MAPP) and the Association for Rubber Products Manufacturers (ARPM), as well as executive director of the American Mold Builders Association (AMBA). Troy has created two national manufacturing magazines and also founded the Benchmarking and Best Practices Conference, which is one of the manufacturing sector's fastest growing and most innovative events.

Troy shares his stories and lessons with audiences internationally from the speaking stage. He also routinely functions as a contributing author for American manufacturing trade publications and studies.

Troy and his wife, Ann, live in Indianapolis, Indiana, and have three children. In his limited free time, he enjoys high-intensity gym workouts, attending rock and roll concerts, and spending time in tropical environments.

For more about Troy, visit troynix.com.

CPSIA information can be obtained
at www.ICGtesting.com
Printed in the USA
BVHW041433260220
573412BV00011B/381